JOYFUL EATING

How to Break Free of Diets and
Make Peace with Your Body

TANSY BOGGON

ISBN: 978-1-6847-0007-3 (sc)
ISBN: 978-1-6847-0006-6 (e)

Library of Congress Control Number: 2019903364

Lulu Publishing Services rev. date: 09/08/2021

Contents

Introduction

You live in a society that has a greater understanding of nutrition and diet than at any time before—a society obsessed with diet and cookbooks, diet programs, diet and protein shakes, fitness magazines, Instagram celebrities and beauty vloggers. You may be able to recall meal plans for various diets and have opinions of foods or diet products you haven't even tried yourself. Despite this, rather than feeling empowered and satisfied with your body, you may instead feel confused and overwhelmed by the contradictory and ever-changing messages. That was certainly the case for me.

In the media, I saw diet proponents flaunt their weight loss successes and others who didn't seem to have any issues with their weight. They appeared to be able to eat whatever their heart desired without gaining weight. I felt like there was something wrong with me for being unable to stick to a diet long enough, or with enough diligence, to replicate their results. I doubted that I had the necessary willpower or motivation to succeed at a diet. I wondered whether women with super-slim and toned bodies just had more self-control than me. I wondered whether I was unlucky with my genetics, or whether my vegetarian diet meant I couldn't achieve the desired tone and definition in muscle.

At the time, I was yet to realise that I wasn't alone in this thinking. I hadn't realised that our diet culture perpetuates dissatisfaction in your body and drives you to embark on diet after diet, luring you in with irresistible promises and enticing before-and-after photos. You may be able to relate. You may have struggled with your weight for years; perhaps you've lost weight only to have it slowly creep back on. Perhaps you've never succeeded at a diet and wonder whether something is wrong with you. Or you may believe that you are eating for health, not weight loss, while still attempting to control your dietary intake and body. Whatever is the case for you, this book will help you to ditch diet rules and diet mentality forever.

Through my journey, it became clear that more consumer information, diet plans or weight loss products wouldn't provide the answer to forming a healthy relationship with food and one's body. For years, I'd searched for the holy grail: the perfect diet or exercise regime to sculpt the body I desired. Like thousands of women, I'd hoped that there was a miracle diet or potion that would be the answer to my body dissatisfaction. Unfortunately, there is not.

I began to realise that I'd been looking in all the wrong places. That it wasn't my lack of willpower or my body that had failed me, but that I'd created unrealistic expectations of myself and my body. I was comparing myself to the images portrayed in the fitness magazines and diet books I was hooked on. I began to understand that diets erode trust in myself and my body. Furthermore, I realised that continuing to search outside of myself was disconnecting me from who I was, and from my body. And as a consequence, contentment with my body always felt out of reach.

The content of this book came together after a decade of reflecting on my inner journey, supplemented with reading, researching, studying nutrition at university, training in coaching, and listening to clients' eating and body concerns. While this is a solid grounding, in no way do I wish to imply that I've discovered all the answers to transform your life and body. Rather, I share information and reflective activities that I believe have the potential to create a substantial change in how you perceive your body—and free you from restriction, deprivation and dieting.

This book is for you if you're fed up with constantly thinking about food and feeling dissatisfied with your body. Let's put an end to the relentless attempts to control your eating and your body.

This book is for you if you've battled to stick to a diet with the necessary diligence to achieve your desired goals. Let's put an end to searching for the perfect diet and struggling to eat right.

This book is for you if you've succeeded on a diet in the past, yet the weight crept back on, or you ended up heavier than when you started. Let's end the feelings of failure, guilt and shame.

However, this is not a diet book! You'll find no meal plans or prescriptions for one right way to eat. You won't be required to count your calorie intake or deprive yourself of foods you enjoy. Plus, you'll find no unrealistic guarantees of weight loss or optimal health.

Throughout this book, you'll be guided to nourish your body in a way that's both enjoyable and sustainable. We'll set out to maximise your feeling of vitality, happiness and contentment, where your happiness is not dependent on the number on the scales or what you ate the day before.

You'll not only discover the philosophy and principles of Joyful Eating, you'll have the opportunity to actively reflect on your own relationship with food and your body, to integrate and experience it for yourself. I invite you to join me on a journey to free yourself from the struggle of deprivation, guilt and shame with eating and with your body. Let's begin.

Your Journey Through This Book

"What a caterpillar calls the end of the world we call a butterfly."

— Eckhart Tolle

Through this book, I aspire to shed light on why you're where you are right now. Why you may find yourself ashamed of your body. Why you may feel confused about what you *should* be eating. Why you may feel like you've failed at dieting or even believe that your body has failed you. And why you may still be searching for the next diet.

I intend for this book to be thought-provoking. Therefore, rather than interpret what I say as an absolute truth or instruction, view it as an invitation to question your own beliefs.

Through my own experience and working with clients, I've come to understand that you're only likely to create the shifts you want to make and only when the time is right. There may be aspects of this book that you can relate to and feel will benefit you. Yet there may be others that don't hold true for you; or you may feel resistance to them because they contradict your beliefs about yourself, your body and your relationship with food. That is perfectly fine. If you were to reread this book in a year, you might find that different aspects resonate than those that do now. So, take it at your own pace. Take the pressure off yourself to achieve a certain goal with this book. Enjoy the journey and the self-realisations that will, hopefully, occur along the way.

Some terminology in this book may seem similar to that used by psychologists. However, I'm not a psychologist. Therefore, there is no intention of replacing a psychologist's role in your healing, especially if you live with a clinically recognised eating or anxiety disorder. Instead, this book is intended to support you in forming a healthier and joyful relationship with food and your body, whether your concerns are clinically recognised or not.

Structure of This Book

I've set this book out in a way that I consider most logical. Although I recommend reading it from start to finish, I understand the desire to jump to the sections that feel most relevant to you right now. Feel free to begin at any section you're drawn to. However, I strongly recommend that you make your way back to the beginning, as some concepts require an understanding of previous information to truly shift your beliefs about your body and food.

Self-Reflection Activities

I hope that you'll not just be a passive observer while reading this book, but engage in self-reflection. Therefore, I've complemented the text with *exercises* called 'Self-Reflection Activities'. These activities are marked with this writing symbol: ✍

Although reading this book without undertaking the Self-Reflection Activities will still be beneficial, it's only through this self-exploration that you will uncover and let go of what is holding you back from contentment with your eating and body. I believe that if you undertake the Self-Reflection Activities, you'll be better able to integrate the Joyful Eating Principles through first-hand experience.

Depending on the type of learner you are and the time you have, you may like to approach this book by either:

- reading one chapter a week and doing the associated Self-Reflection Activities during that week, providing you time to reflect and determine what holds true for you; or
- reading the entire book, allowing the entirety of the content to *sink in,* before then doing the Self-Reflection Activities in whatever order feels right for you.

Either way, I suggest you do no more than one or two Self-Reflection Activities per week so that you can reflect on them during the week, observing your behaviour and the thoughts that arise.

You can work through the Self-Reflection Activities in the companion Workbook, which you can download for free at www.joyfuleatingnutrition. com/book. Alternatively, you could dedicate a notebook or journal to the activities.

In your Workbook or journal, you could also include recipes you enjoy, articles, images, sketches or doodles; whatever helps to make it uniquely yours and a useful tool that you want to come back to regularly. Your Workbook or journal is likely to become an invaluable resource that you can skim through every year or so to reinforce what you've learned.

✍ Take stock of your current relationship with food and your body

Before you read further, now is a good time to assess where you are in your relationship with food and your body. That way, you have something written that you can come back to and reassess how your thoughts around food and your body has changed through this journey, and identify areas that require further attention. This self-reflection may also help you determine where you want to start in this book if you wish to skip ahead.

You'll find the assessment tool in Appendix 3: *Take stock of your current relationship with food and your body.*

In no way is this tool a test; there are no right or wrong answers. Therefore, be truthful in your answers, so that you can accurately determine your priorities and notice any changes attained through reading and undertaking the Self-Reflection Activities in this book.

PART I

Establishing a Foundation for Joyful Eating

1

Unravelling Your Food and Body Story

"Let go of your story so the Universe can write a new one for you."

— Marianne Williamson

Your food and body narrative—the story you tell yourself—forms the lens through which you see your body and relate with food. It's formed by the events and experiences that have contributed to your current thoughts and beliefs about yourself, your body and your relationship with food.

Shortly I'll invite you to reflect on your own food and body story, but before I do, let me share my own. After all, it's what has compelled me to write this book. My story is founded on how I perceive the world. It is unique to me, just as your narrative is to you.

My Food and Body Story

My maternal grandmother struggled with her weight her entire adult life and sadly died at far too young an age, due to what many in the medical field would consider obesity-related issues. As one of eight children and growing up with financial hardship and an alcoholic father, she had a diminished sense of self-worth. As a beautiful young woman, she married my grandfather. He was an insecure man who inflated his ego by putting her down. His regular verbal abuse fuelled her sense of worthlessness. My mother tells of coming home from school to find her mother, still robed in her dressing gown, sitting on the couch in the same position she had been in when my mother had left for school. To prevent a *blow up* between my grandmother and grandfather, my mother, as a child and teenager, would wash the dishes, put things away, brush my grandmother's hair and help her to get dressed.

Even as a child, it was evident to me that my grandmother ate food to numb out from her painful life circumstance. Her weight fluctuated as she was either on or off a diet. She struggled with depression and diabetes, which contributed largely to her death.

Diabetes and *obesity* were prevalent in my mother's family; her early experiences and knowledge of this formed the foundation of her relationship with food and her body. It's therefore understandable that she had an immense fear of gaining weight and prioritised controlling her dietary intake.

When we were children, my mother made sure my sister and I were aware of our genetic propensity for obesity and our family traits of compulsive, emotional eating and overeating. As inspiration and reinforcement that we had to control our weight, my mother would often recount the story of a cousin who turned his life around, reversing his Type II diabetes through diet and exercise. Our mother made it clear that health was a choice and within our control. Her core method of controlling her weight was through her food intake.

As children, we ate incredibly healthily compared to most households. We ate a vegetarian diet comprised of ample wholegrains, legumes, nuts, seeds, fruits and vegetables. *Junk food* was a rarity. Our treats were homemade cakes, cookies, pancakes or popcorn. In spite of our wholesome diet, my mother would often forgo certain indulgences or make modifications to her servings to reduce fat or calories.

Despite their contrast—my grandmother, who was *obese*, unwell and unhappy, versus my mother, who prioritised healthy eating—I could see that they'd both struggled. My grandmother often lost the battle with her weight and seemed out of control with her eating. My mother, on the other hand, lived with her weight constantly in front of mind and persistently attempted to restrict and control her eating. Bearing witness to these contrasting relationships with food and body, I didn't want to deprive myself of delicious foods like my mother, although I also feared the potentiality of gaining excess weight like my grandmother.

After leaving home, I attempted to control my weight by restricting what I ate during the week, reducing my portions throughout the day and occasionally skipping meals. I'd work out like crazy up to two hours a day, six days a week, in addition to riding my bicycle to work. Despite my intensive exercise regime, I often only ate a small handful of fruit and nuts for lunch. So, it's no surprise that by dinner time I was often so hungry I'd mindlessly devour a huge bowl of pasta and cheese.

On the weekends I'd frequently eat excessive quantities of what I perceived to be *treat foods*. I'd devour entire containers of ice cream, large bags of chips and family size blocks of chocolate with my then-partner. Although I immensely enjoyed these foods, each time I ate them it was in a way as if I'd never have them again. Essentially, I spent the week starving myself and the weekend gorging.

Yet my body just didn't measure up. I so badly wanted a flat, bikini-worthy stomach as depicted in women's fitness magazines and I envied the girls who could confidently jump around in their sports bra in aerobics classes. The bikini body as depicted in magazines never eventuated. I hadn't realised it at the time, but this wasn't the path to feeling content with my body.

In my late twenties, I travelled with my then-partner for ten months. Without the routine of work, it was hard to maintain an exercise regime and a sense of control over my eating. Inevitably, I gained a few kilos and increased a dress size.

During our travels, our relationship of eleven years came to an end. This emotional upheaval further increased my eating for comfort. After returning to Australia, single and heavier than ever before, I realised that I couldn't sustain my previous pattern of feast and famine. I decided that I had to try something other than depriving myself on weekdays and then overeating on the weekends.

In place of restricting specific foods, I focused on enjoying everything I ate. I realised that I ate some foods in excess primarily because I believed that they were *bad* or *naughty*, rather than because I truly enjoyed them. I became aware of the foods I did enjoy versus the foods I ate just because I perceived them as a treat.

With this new focus, I chose to make or purchase the most delicious and gourmet version of the foods I enjoyed. So, rather than my food purchases being about what was the best value for money, I purchased what would satisfy me and bring me the most joy. For example, a tub of ice cream may well be better value for money than a chocolate-coated ice cream on a stick. However, the chocolate-coated ice cream was more than sufficient to satisfy my desire for ice cream. And at that stage, if a tub of ice cream was in the freezer I'd compulsively go for more, even if I wasn't hungry or enjoying it: I would eat it simply because it was there.

I no longer focused on controlling my portions, but rather on being fully aware of the experience of eating, and my hunger and fullness cues. I was turning my attention inwards. So, rather than external cues such as time of day or meal plans dictating my eating, it was guided by my internal sensations of hunger, along with the sensory experience of eating. I began to relish food and savour every mouthful. I could enjoy tiramisu without eating as if it would be the last slice I'd ever have. I didn't realise it at the time, but I was embracing what I now call *Joyful Eating*.

Despite the shift that was occurring in my relationship with food, it certainly wasn't smooth sailing. For many years, I continued to over-exercise to maintain a *healthy figure*. Although I'd switched from obsessing over the *quantity* of food I ate, such as calories, portions and macronutrient

4

proportions, to the *quality* of what I ate, I continued to attempt to control my diet.

At that time I believed (as so many diet proponents proclaim) that eating specific foods, prepared in specific ways, was the answer to body satisfaction and health. I researched and attempted traditional diets, raw food, metabolic diets, nutritional typing, blood type, low carbohydrate, sugar-free, gluten-free, juice cleanses, supplements and a number of popular and largely unfounded diets. These diets lured me in with declarations that restrictive calorie diets don't work, but these diet plans *did*.

I can now admit that the raw food and gluten-free diet I faithfully followed for some years was driven predominantly by superficial reasons and the illusion they would provide *optimal health*. Despite the alluring before-and-after photos and promises of enduring health, these diets were just as restrictive and complicated as any weight loss diet. I learned through self-exploration, and later through my studies in nutrition, that there is no perfect approach to eating for health.

Then in 2009, a substantial shift in my perception of food and my body occurred when I undertook training as a coach and facilitator with ZoneHigh, an organisation focused on helping people reach their full potential. This training helped me understand and experience for myself how my state of being and beliefs influence my success, happiness and fulfilment. I began to practise techniques to heighten my awareness in each moment. I noticed how this new awareness enabled me to *hear* what my body truly required and spontaneously take steps to nurture myself, unlike my previous controlling and stressful approach.

So, I started to let go of concerning myself about bulges here or there and turned my focus to feeling alive. I began to see how my rules and beliefs didn't serve me but instead eroded trust in my own body.

Letting go of the need to control my body, I discovered that I didn't need to exercise so intensely to maintain my health and fitness. Rather than exercising to burn fat or sculpt my body, I now choose movement that enables me to feel strong, flexible and energetic, as well as movement that reduces aches and pains that result from sitting for long periods. No longer do I feel the need to push my body to achieve results. If I'm tired, I may rest, gently stretch or go for a slow walk. In comparison, years ago I'd drag myself to the gym, workout too hard and potentially end up too sore to work-out for days, often coming home with a seemingly uncontrollable appetite.

I discovered that I didn't need to restrict and control my eating to eat *right* for me, but rather quieten my mind and tune into how my body responds to what I eat. Along with this, I accepted that I don't control how my body responds to the foods I eat or the exercise I do.

Once I dropped my diet and food rules, I didn't crave what I'd previously perceived as unhealthy foods so much. I can sit and enjoy a slice of tiramisu without the voice in my head driving me to eat more, telling me that there is more in the fridge. I can now tune into my body and decide whether I will eat more or stop eating, based on internal cues.

I've let go of using external measures such as the scales or tape measure to assess my success or dictate my happiness. These were never great motivators for me anyway. If I weighed myself and there had been no change, or I'd gained weight, I'd feel like a failure and consequently unmotivated: as it wasn't worth the effort to continue. If I'd lost weight, I'd think, *now I have lost the weight, I'd better keep it off.* As a consequence, I'd feel greater pressure to keep up the restrictive eating, and at times I'd push myself even harder to attain my goals. Inevitably, I'd relapse to my familiar and comfortable eating patterns and exercise regime, as the hard work became overwhelming or unsustainable.

Now, I eat (or don't eat) foods available to me based on how I feel in the moment and with an awareness of how certain foods may make me feel. Sometimes when I eat what I'd previously perceived as a treat food, I can take a bite or two and think, *that's enough.* Other times I may think, *this isn't as delicious as I thought it would be,* or *it's not what my body wants right now.* There is rarely the thought, *I shouldn't eat this,* or *it's so unfair that I can't have this.* I no longer feel guilt for what I've eaten or a need to compensate for my eating.

My journey was gradual as I reflected and considered many disciplines to shed light on my relationship with food and my body. Later in my journey and as I began to support others, I discovered non-diet approach, intuitive eating, mindful eating and Health at Every Size. Although these were not instrumental in my journey, they align with the approach I took and share in this book.

Through *listening* to my body and emotions, my relationship with food and my body is now far more joyful and balanced. I acknowledge that my relationship with food and my body is constantly evolving. I believe it's a lifelong journey. Over the years my circumstances will change, as too will my body. However, I no longer feel the pressure to control my body. I used to believe it necessary to criticise my body to control my weight. I've learnt that this is untrue and that the opposite may be true.

As a consequence of my journey and what I've learned along the way, I now aspire to help others like my grandmother, my mother, myself and you, end the struggle with food and discover how body acceptance and embracing the joy of eating can free you of dieting, guilt and shame. I'm delighted that you're here to join me.

Your Food and Body Story

Perhaps you can relate to my story, maybe not. You have your own unique story and beliefs that shape your relationship with food and your body. I encourage you to take some time, now, before you read this book further, to reflect on and record your food and body narrative.

✍ Your food and body story

Write your food and body story in your Workbook or journal. It can be as short or long as you like. Take your time with it. You may find that writing some dot points and then going for a walk or doing a chore around the house enables you to reflect, and your story to fully unfold.

If you don't know where to start, you might like to consider the following prompts:

- your memories of food as a child
- your parents, grandparents, other relatives or influential peoples relationship with food and dieting
- food and diet *wisdom* passed on by friends, family, colleagues, social media and diets you've attempted
- when you first developed weight concerns
- past diets you've been on
- fluctuations in your weight
- your feelings and thoughts about dieting or your weight
- how you've felt when you have or have not achieved results on a diet
- your beliefs about food and diet
- changes in your beliefs about food and diet

Through your narrative, you may begin to uncover the origins of your current beliefs about food and your body, and see recurring patterns that have presented themselves throughout your life. You'll have the opportunity to come back to the beliefs that form the basis of your relationship with food and your body throughout this book.

Is Your Story Based on a Lie?

Through this book, you'll discover—as I did—that many of your beliefs about food and your body are untrue. Your beliefs may have enabled you to cope or served you for a certain period. However, believing these stories only continue to cause you pain and suffering.

Let's debunk the diet, food and body beliefs that no longer serve you, beginning with the most fundamental lie that keeps you trapped in diet mentality and body dissatisfaction: the lie that you can control and manage your weight through dieting.

2

Debunk the Diet Myth

*"True kindness has no calories. True kindness is deciding right now that
you deserve to feel fabulous—even if you never lose another pound."*

— Geneen Roth

Given that dieting is so accepted and ingrained in western culture, it's
possible that you've never questioned whether it's the most effective way
to achieve and maintain a *healthy* weight or good health. So, let's explore
why diets are so alluring: why you may have spent much of your life either
on a diet or thinking about the next diet. And quite simply, why diets
don't work.

Let's take a moment to define what's meant by the word *diet*. It has
two meanings. The first is what a person or animal habitually eats. So,
you may say, 'I eat a vegetarian diet', or 'a lion's diet comprises of raw
meat'. The second meaning, which is the focus of this book, involves the
restriction of food to promote weight loss or other health goals. So, you
may say, 'I'm on a diet to lose five kilos', or 'I've started a diet to reduce
inflammation'.

In respect to the latter, diets are short-term prescriptions or guidelines for
weight loss or other health objectives. Weight loss diets often prescribe
specific proportions of macronutrients—fat, protein and carbohydrates—as

they differ in energy composition, absorption and metabolism. The main rationale is that the less energy you consume, the more your body will draw on fat stores for energy, thus promoting weight loss.

This sounds straightforward and logical, and some diet proponents believe it is. They declare that you simply need to *eat less, exercise more.* Unfortunately—and you'll know this first-hand if you've attempted diets or other weight loss programs—it's not that simple. If it were, you wouldn't need to read this book, nor would there be a surplus of books on the topics of weight loss and dieting.

The Diet Cycle

Allow me to introduce you to the *diet cycle.* The diet cycle reveals how you can become trapped in the on-again-off-again cycle of repeating diet, after diet, after diet.

i. The dissatisfaction

The impulse to diet begins with dissatisfaction with your body, weight, health or eating behaviour. This dissatisfaction may originate from internal beliefs and self-perception or from external influences, such as the mass media telling you that you should be a certain weight or size to be healthy, attractive or desirable. It is dissatisfaction that initiates the diet cycle, and it is dissatisfaction that keeps it going.

ii. The allure of diets

Diets lure you in with promises of unbelievable results, if only you can maintain the immense discipline to restrict and control your eating. You may begin a diet with enthusiasm and excitement in anticipation of these promised results. However, if you're anything like the majority of people, this enthusiasm and excitement soon wane—possibly within a day, a week or a month—as the hard work of dieting and deprivation sets in.

iii. The insatiable hunger and temptation

The immense restriction and deprivation required for most diets eventually leads to an insatiable hunger and preoccupation with foods that are forbidden on the diet. You may be able to ignore your body's signals and your incessant thoughts about food for some time, and possibly attempt to control your eating even further. However, it is likely that you eventually *give in* to the overpowering hunger and temptation. If not, you may find yourself on a path to disordered eating.

iv. The floodgates to eating

Eventually, you *give in* and eat, as that's exactly what your body is designed to do in times of famine: drive you to eat to restore energy balance. As a result, your subsequent eating may seem excessive, leading you to believe that you've lost control of your eating. And if your weight hasn't reduced, you may feel you have failed at dieting. Consequently, you may feel immense guilt and shame, which brings you full circle to feeling dissatisfaction with your body, weight, health or eating behaviour.

Free yourself from the Diet Cycle

You might relate to the entire diet cycle or certain stages more than others. It may be that you feel out of control more often than not. Conversely, you may restrict and deprive yourself more than you lose control over your eating. Or you may go through the complete diet cycle every few days, month or year.

Right now, you may be ready to quit dieting, as you can see how in the past you've been trapped in the diet cycle and you just want it to end. Or, you might require more evidence and explanation to quit dieting. Here you go.

Why Your Body Rejects Diets

Despite the widely-held belief that you can control your body through dieting, your body fights against diets in various ways, sabotaging your efforts. Let's take a closer look at the ways your body rejects diets.

Diets require a calorie deficit

Weight loss diets require a *calorie deficit*; that is, the consumption of fewer calories than required to maintain your current weight. The calorie deficit of most diets is even less than would be required to maintain the weight you set as a target. The reason: to create rapid weight loss.

A calorie deficit seems logical if you presume your weight is the result of the balance between energy consumed and energy expended. However, there are physiological and psychological effects that make sticking to a diet and maintaining weight loss—should you succeed on a diet—very difficult.

It's difficult to stick to a diet because your body *screams* at you to restore the calorie deficit (as you're essentially starving yourself). It doesn't matter if you're clinically overweight or have been consuming excessive calories, your body responds to the substantial reduction in calories, not your body weight.

A cornerstone study that demonstrates this is *The Minnesota Starvation Experiment, 1944-1945*. This study explored the physical and mental response of dietary restriction on 36 healthy young men during World War II (1,2). It intended to determine the most appropriate diet to reinstate the weight of starved prisoners of war once they returned home.

The study firstly required the starvation of these men, so that the researchers could then compare dietary rehabilitation strategies. The men received a diet of only two meals a day, totalling 1570 calories. Astonishingly, the calories consumed was higher than most modern weight loss diets! This fact reinforces that when you diet, you are starving your body.

Unlike *some* modern diets, the diet in this study was not nutritionally balanced. However, a similar response to starvation and the associated decline in strength and energy is what you'd experience if you went on a diet of insufficient caloric intake.

Although the men in the study had no prior issues with weight or food, on the starvation diet, they became obsessed with food. They lost interest in political affairs, world events, romance and sex. Food became their overwhelming priority. Some men reported reading cookbooks and would stare at pictures of food.

You may relate to going on a diet and feeling like all you can think about is food. And unlike those men, today you can watch *food porn* by way of cooking shows!

Cheating the starvation diet became an issue among the men, as they reported an almost uncontrollable urge to seek food. How similar is this to secret, compulsive or binge eating? The hunger and preoccupation with food that dieting creates also triggers an uncontrollable urge to eat (3). Unfortunately, you may blame this urge on your lack of motivation or willpower, when in fact it's an underlying biological drive for survival.

The Minnesota Starvation Experiment reinforces that the deprivation and restriction required on modern diets is something that most people can only keep up for a short period. Although it may be argued that the men in the study were of a healthy weight before they started and so may not represent overweight individuals, dieting is prevalent these days among people who are of a healthy weight. Often, they desire weight loss to fit into *that dress* or adjust slightly to the weight they were way back when. No matter your weight before dieting, restrictive dieting results in insatiable hunger and obsession with food, making sticking to a diet extremely difficult, if not impossible, for any meaningful length of time.

Diets slow your metabolism

When you go on a calorie restrictive diet, your body responds by slowing down your metabolism to conserve energy. This is known as the *starvation response*. The starvation response is a primitive response to protect your body during times of famine. In the starvation response, your metabolism slows, reducing your heart rate, lean muscle mass and the water content in your muscles (1,4). These changes enable your body to hold onto fat and conserve the calories you consume.

Quite simply, when in a caloric deficit your body compensates by burning fewer calories. To support this theory, a study on mice found that when food is scarce, as is the case when dieting, the brain triggers neurons that prevent burning calories (5). Consistent with this, the lead author of a Cambridge Institute of Public Health study, Dr Blouet said, "our findings suggest that a group of neurons in the brain coordinate appetite and energy expenditure, and can turn a switch on and off to burn or spare calories depending on what's available in the environment. If food is available, they make us eat, and if food is scarce, they turn our body into saving mode and stop us from burning fat" (6).

Regrettably, your body doesn't know the difference between a self-induced calorie restriction, aka diet, or a famine. Your body responds to the scarcity of food and energy on a diet to maintain your current weight, even if it's not the weight you'd like to be. There is no way to tell your body that it's okay to lose weight, that food is plentiful and that you are starving yourself by choice. Therefore, your biology ensures that dieting has little effect on your weight long-term. It thus explains why you may have experienced or heard others talk about their weight 'plateauing' on a diet.

A further implication of dieting is that *weight loss* does not imply *fat loss*. The initial weight loss experienced on a diet is a consequence of metabolic responses, rather than fat loss. You can lose approximately 400 g in glucose stores (in the form of glycogen from the liver and muscle) and 1200 g of water when you initially restrict your energy intake. So, although the results for the first two weeks of a diet can look promising, your weight can plateau because the initial results were more to do with water loss than fat loss. The water loss from your muscles further reduces your metabolism, contributing to the weight plateau. And the thing is, the water loss will be regained rapidly as soon as you resume eating normally.

Diets contribute to weight gain

Even if you persist with a diet or succeed at it, because your energy intake during the diet is likely substantially less than required to maintain the weight you were aiming for, once you start eating as you do normally, the weight is likely to creep back on. Post-diet weight gain has been demonstrated time and time again by countless studies and anecdotal evidence.

It is widely believed that 95 percent of dieters will put the weight back on after a diet, and often gain more weight than before dieting. A review of nine scientific studies that examined the relationship between dieting and weight gain found that dieting or dietary restraint was consistently associated with increased risk of weight gain (7). A study of over four thousand individual twins found that the twin who was the most frequent dieter was more susceptible to weight gain (8). And a weight difference between twins was evident with just one diet! Another study, in 1995, went so far as to say that weight loss interventions only produce short-term losses followed by weight regain, and that "no current treatments appear capable of producing permanent weight loss" (9). Down under, Australian population data demonstrates that dieting to lose weight is a contributor to future obesity and weight gain (10). While a review of long-term outcomes of calorie-restriction diets found that one- to two-thirds of dieters regained more weight than they lost on their diets (11).

This latter review adds further insult to injury by not finding consistent evidence that short-term weight loss contributes to significant health improvements. So, not only is depriving and restricting yourself ineffective in achieving and maintaining weight loss, it is ineffective in improving health.

The weight gain after dieting—known as the *rebound effect*—can be rapid. This is not only due to reinstating glycogen and water stores, but because the body lays down fat in anticipation of the next food scarcity.

Furthermore, the body stays in the starvation response long after a diet has ended, due to the loss of muscle mass and changes in the hormones involved in the regulation of body weight (4,12,13). Unfortunately, these hormonal changes can continue for over a year after you've ceased a diet. A study by Australian researchers on fifty overweight and obese patients found that hormones and appetite were significantly altered one year after undertaking the weight loss program, even once participants restored their pre-program weight (12). Similarly, a study on obese rats found that after a diet to stimulate weight loss, their appetite was elevated and did not revert to pre-weight loss appetite levels within one year (14).

The *Minnesota Starvation Experiment* revealed that when the men could eat unrestricted after the experiment ended, they ate considerably more calories than they did before the experiment; and in some cases, nearly three times the before-experiment calorie consumption in a single day! For many months, the men reported having a sensation of hunger that they couldn't satisfy no matter how much they ate. All the men gained more weight than they had before the experiment. Although with time, they eventually resumed their pre-experiment weight.

As previously mentioned, the men in this study had no prior body or weight issues, and no reported resistance to the weight overshooting that occurred before stabilisation to their pre-experiment weight (15). However, if you've struggled with your weight and eating, regaining that weight—or gaining more weight than before a diet—can be disheartening and potentially lead you to start yet another diet before your body can achieve balance.

Your setpoint weight

If you diet again within one year, your body is unlikely to achieve a balanced weight. You are likely to *swing* between losing weight and gaining it back, like a pendulum swinging from side to side. The centre of this pendulum would constitute what is known as your *setpoint weight*: a weight range to which you're genetically predisposed (16,17). Your setpoint weight is as unique as your height or shoe size.

Your body regulates body weight by a gland in the brain called the hypothalamus. It's believed that the hypothalamus ensures that changes in metabolism and behaviour counter an increase or decrease in either food intake or energy expenditure (17,18). So, in a healthy person, overeating is followed by increased thermogenesis (aka body temperature, metabolism and energy expenditure) to burn the excess calories (19,18). On the other hand, increased energy expenditure, as in the case of strenuous exercise, stimulates increased food intake.

Individuals who don't consume enough to maintain their current weight tend to experience a slowing of their basal metabolism to conserve energy, along with an intensification of hunger to promote eating. Therefore, attempting to keep your body weight below its setpoint through restricting energy consumption is a never-ending struggle: your body will constantly fight back to restore the natural weight range for your body.

You might wonder why, since your body has a setpoint weight range, dieting leads to weight gain rather than your body reverting to your genetically-predetermined setpoint. It could be that the weight gain experienced on ceasing a diet is only temporary and that your body wasn't allowed sufficient time to *settle* before you embarked on another diet. Moreover, your setpoint weight appears to be adjustable to other *settling points* by mechanisms other than the hypothalamus, including fat cells, nutrients, dietary composition, hormones, neural pathways, brain nuclei and neurotransmitters (20,5,21,15,16). Therefore, it is possible that diets may result in changes in your body that can temporarily or permanently alter your setpoint weight range.

Diets lead to weight cycling

A fluctuating weight, also termed *weight cycling*, has health consequences that may be more detrimental to your health than maintaining a stable weight. Research has demonstrated that repeated weight loss and weight gain raises blood cortisol (stress hormone), promotes inflammation throughout the body, and increases the risk of metabolic and cardiovascular diseases (22). Surprisingly, these risk factors are more prevalent in people of normal weight who yo-yo diet, such as dieting each year to obtain that elusive *beach body*, than in individuals that maintain a relatively constant weight, even if within the *overweight* or *obese* weight range (23,7).

It follows that if weight cycling is associated with increased disease risk, recommending weight loss may potentially be a greater public health issue than obesity. This realisation has given rise to the *Health at Every Size®* movement, which advocates that people can adopt healthy lifestyle changes to improve their health at any size, and that weight is not an accurate measure of health (24). This movement suggests that it's not a person's weight, but lifestyle factors that are better predictors of health. At any weight or size, you can eat, move and live in ways that nourish your body, with or without weight loss.

Thinking, *I'll lose weight and then adopt healthier lifestyle behaviours*, is also flawed. Adopting unhealthy methods to lose weight, such as starving yourself, consuming diet pills, replacing nourishing meals with shakes, depriving your body of energy and nutrition, or punishing it with gruelling exercise regimes, does nothing to promote good health. Rather, they do more to set your weight swinging on that metaphorical pendulum.

Diets promote disordered eating

Dieting can be a precursor for disordered thinking about food and your body, and thus eating disorders, such as binge eating disorder, bulimia and anorexia. Research indicates that the prevalence of eating disorders would be substantially less if dieting and body image issues were not so rampant in society (25,26). A three-year study of Australian students, who were aged 14-15 years at the onset of the study, demonstrated that moderate dieters are five times more likely than non-dieters to develop an eating disorder (27).

Eating disorders involve a complex interplay between physiological and psychological factors, so recovery is far more complicated than simply ditching diet mentality. It requires the support of a multi-disciplinary team of specialised therapists and health care providers. However, I mention these disorders here to highlight yet another reason how diets erode your relationship with food and your body, without the supposed health benefits.

Why Your Mind Rejects Diets

Not only does your body resist dieting through immense hunger, slowing your metabolism, weight gain, weight cycling, and increasing your risk of disordered eating, your mind also rejects diets. Diets set your behaviours and emotions swinging on that metaphorical pendulum, from restrictive dieting—where you feel in control—to excessive eating—where you feel completely out of control. Let's now explore the psychological reasons that diets sabotage your weight loss efforts and your ability to maintain a stable weight.

Diets require body dissatisfaction

Despite marketing messages and government campaigns to inspire you to lose weight, these messages do more to create stigma around weight and potentially amplify an already negative self-perception. You are taught that constantly identifying faults with your body, or yourself, will motivate you to change. However, you can't hate yourself thin.

Weight stigma

Sadly, although shame and blame are certainly not effective means of motivation (discussed in more detail later), health professionals frequently contribute to weight stigmatisation (28,29,30). A published review of scientific journals confirmed that many healthcare providers hold strong negative attitudes and stereotypes about *obese* people, which influences their interpersonal behaviour and decision-making (31). Weight stigma can contribute to overweight patients receiving substandard care because their ailments are assumed to be either weight or self-induced. These patients may avoid care as they dread having their weight mentioned at a consultation. Consequently, weight stigma can perpetuate avoidance of seeking medical support, mistrust of health professionals or poor adherence to prescriptions… all of which can have considerable health implications.

Contrary to the common perception that apportioning blame on the individual will serve to motivate them, this doesn't seem to be the case. Weight stigma has been shown to impact a patient's self-esteem, depression and quality of life (32,33). Frequent exposure to weight stigmatisation has been demonstrated to perpetuate unhealthy lifestyle behaviours and obesity, rather than prevent or reverse it (33). A study of 100 female undergraduates on motivation to exercise found that weight stigma results in a decrease in physical activity, not an increase, as may be expected (34). Therefore, although the unsolicited advice to lose weight may be intended to motivate a patient into action, it does more to intensify feelings of shame than inspire healthy lifestyle changes.

But isn't being obese, unhealthy and being thin, healthy?

The perception that being thin is healthy is simply untrue; you cannot determine someone's health by appearance alone. You could be your ideal weight, or what is considered either a healthy weight by medical metrics, yet eat insufficient quantities of food to meet nutritional requirements, eat negligible fresh fruits and vegetables, and do no exercise. In this case, you may be privileged because your genetics allow you to adopt unhealthy behaviours and maintain what is perceived as a healthy weight; though this does not make you healthy.

Interestingly, scientific research indicates that being underweight is equally as unhealthy as being overweight. A study of over 900,000 individuals found a correlation of diminished markers of health for individuals at either end of the body mass index (BMI). Both underweight and overweight individuals had an increased probability of diminished health and associated mortality (35). The thing is, lifestyle diseases develop in the absence of obesity, and being what is considered *obese* provides no guarantee of developing any specific health condition.

So, your weight provides absolutely no guarantee of good health, illness or mortality. It merely indicates a probability based on correlations at the population level. Correlations do not prove which factor causes which: whether obesity causes specific health conditions, whether certain health conditions cause obesity, or whether some other unexplored factors cause both obesity and specific health conditions. Quite simply, you can't be certain that health concerns are the result of your weight. Nor do you know whether weight loss will reverse them. Scientific research indicates negligible improvements in health after weight loss (36), suggesting that it's not the magic bullet to good health that you've been led to believe.

In recent years, there has also been debate as to whether obesity is in fact a disease. Obesity is often correlated with an increased risk of illness and disease, but it is a risk factor, not a disease in its own right. Pathologising obesity places more emphasis on weight and solidifies the perception that weight loss to an ideal weight is the fundamental requirement for good health. Deeming obesity a disease may encourage the adoption of rapid and extreme measures to lose weight, such as meal replacements, supplements, medications and surgeries, rather than lifestyle changes to improve health and quality of life.

Diets can be stressful

The incessant thinking that occurs when you're on a diet—about what and when to eat, what you should or shouldn't have eaten—can be stressful. Dieting has been demonstrated to have negative emotional consequences contributing to depression, anxiety, decreased self-esteem, nervousness and irritability (37). It comes as no surprise then that dieters are more likely to eat when stressed or to eat emotionally than non-dieters (38).

Stress plays a significant role in your health and body weight. The stress of dieting can sabotage your efforts for good health by stimulating the stress response in your body; more on this later.

Diets promote 'the last supper' effect

Have you ever decided or declared that your new diet starts on Monday, only to then find yourself justifying having seconds, finishing off the bottle of wine, or having a dessert? You may have thought, *I'll eat chocolate now, as it will be the last I can have once I start this diet.* Eating in anticipation of future restriction is known as the *last supper effect.*

The last supper effect is a common occurrence among dieters. A study of female university students found that participants who were expected

22

to diet for one week ate significantly more in a taste-rating task than the control group, who weren't told they would go on a diet (39,7).

In addition to eating in response to anticipated restriction, the dread of upcoming restriction can fuel eating as a final *hurrah* before the hard work begins. You may believe you require a treat to congratulate yourself for beginning a diet or to mark the commencement.

Up till now, you may have believed that this anticipatory eating is a personal failing. Not at all, it is a completely natural response to fear of future deprivation and restriction (40). It's not that you can't trust yourself around certain foods, it's more that declaring you will stop eating certain foods can intensify your desire for them.

Diets initiate food obsession

If you tell yourself you can't eat a specific food, you may unintentionally draw your thoughts and attention to it. In psychology, this focus on what you don't want to think about is termed the *bear phenomenon* (41). It occurs when you tell yourself not to think about, say bears, and an image of a bear comes into your mind. When you're told or say to yourself to stop thinking about something, you have put the thought of that very thing into your mind.

You can observe these thoughts in action with small children when they're riding a tricycle along a footpath. Although their mind tells them to avoid the oncoming walkers, because their attention is on the walkers ahead, they begin to veer towards them. They head towards the very thing they're trying to avoid.

Similarly, when you place your attention on what you don't want, say foods you've forbidden yourself to eat, it can feel as though it's all you can think about. Telling yourself you 'won't eat chocolate for the next week' does more to stimulate thoughts and a desire for chocolate, than actually prevent you eating it.

Diets demand considerable self-control

Because diets intensify hunger and temptation, you may believe that you require greater self-control and discipline. However, it's not a lack of control that derails your diet efforts. It is your innate response to hunger, deprivation and restriction that leads to what you might consider out-of-control eating. Your body is responding exactly as it should; although it may not be what you want. Later I'll share why you don't need greater control, willpower or motivation to nourish and care for your body.

Ditch the Diet Mentality

The evidence is clear—diets do not work. Some people may have *achieved* results on a diet, revealing before-and-after photos on social media or in magazines. However, they are an anomaly, not the norm.

I acknowledge how daunting it can be to stop dieting, especially if you've lost weight on a diet before, or dieting is the only way you feel you can control your eating. I've heard people say that they've successfully lost weight on a specific diet before and will do it again this New Year. Think about it: if you have to do a diet again, did it work? If you lost weight to put it back on by the following Christmas, what sort of success is that? It's time to liberate yourself from the diet cycle.

The it's not a diet, diet

You may feel that the issues I've raised about dieting don't apply to you, as you've already ditched calorie-restrictive diets for a *healthy lifestyle change*. Although many healthy lifestyle programs state, 'it's not a diet', the belief that being overweight is unhealthy remains. Weight loss is frequently listed as a health benefit alongside increasing muscle mass and energy, or cleansing and healing your body. The insidious message is that weight loss is a possibility on the so-named program, and that weight loss is healthy. These lifestyle programs can provide a glimmer of hope that when your health improves, you'll achieve a *healthy* weight. If you believe that weight loss is healthy, this logic will remain: you have not ditched the diet mentality.

On face value, aspiring for health can seem to be an improvement over adopting extreme and potentially harmful methods in the pursuit of weight loss. However, switching your goal to healthy lifestyle changes can be just as restrictive and stressful. Often the eating plans or lifestyle changes that replace calorie counting involve cutting out entire food groups, require diligent meal planning or eating that's substantially different from social norms. Not only do these lifestyle changes often come with stringent rules, but they can also provoke anxiety and be socially isolating. It's even possible that you believe your friends are attempting to poison you with their grandmother's fruit cake or other *harmful substances* such as gluten, sugar, honey or as is the case with some popular diets, bananas.

No matter how alluring the names and the stated benefits of many popular lifestyle programs, they are typically diets by another guise. You really are on a diet if you either think or declare:

- *'x' food is better than 'y' food*
- *'I shouldn't eat that' or 'I should eat this'*
- *I must avoid gluten/sugar/carbs/wheat/legumes/buffets/drinks with colleagues, etc.*
- *I can have cheat days*
- *I'm not doing it right*
- *I need to do my 60-minute exercise session no matter how tired I am, and make that 90 minutes if I've eaten too much*
- *I need to fill up on salad or a piece of fruit at the start of every meal so that I don't eat too much*
- *I shouldn't eat after 8 pm*
- *if it's not organic/clean/paleo/raw etc., it's not good for me*

The thing is, when you retain the slightest belief, or hope, that you can control your eating or your body's responses, you are still on a diet.

To completely ditch diet mentality, it's important to understand that:

- there are no guarantees that the way you eat or your lifestyle changes will influence your weight or prevent ill health;
- weight loss does not guarantee that you'll become healthier; and
- you can improve your health without changing your weight.

The myth of optimal health

It's not only people that are dissatisfied with their weight or are unwell that strive for good health. Many people who are *healthy* want to achieve *optimal health*. I strived for optimal health until I began to question: What is optimal health? Do I control my health? How does believing so impact my life? Let me explain by firstly clarifying what health is.

The World Health Organization defines health as, "a state of complete physical, mental, and social well-being and not merely the absence of disease or infirmity" (42). So, health goes way beyond your physicality or what you weigh. It is a consequence of a complicated interplay between physical, mental and emotional factors.

Although it is possible to define health, it is hard to quantify. A cardiologist may gauge your health differently from your family doctor, gynaecologist, nutritionist, psychologist or personal trainer. Though they may each assess your health against scientifically validated markers of health, these markers are based on compartmentation of your body and so don't necessarily represent a complete picture of your health and well-being.

Even with our advancements in medical technology and markers of health, scientists and health professionals need to determine where to *draw a line in the sand* to conclude that, for instance, this BMI, blood pressure or blood cholesterol is healthy or not. Therefore, health is subjective. It depends on the markers of health measured; the perspective of the scientists that define and develop markers of health; each health professionals' choice of markers for assessment of health; and an individual's self-perception of well-being. *Optimal health* is an even more subjective concept, as it goes beyond well-being and the absence of disease, to functioning at your peak state… whatever that is?

Now, I'm not suggesting that you ignore health assessments or avoid having regular medical check-ups. But recognise that health does not exist in absolutes—of healthy and unhealthy—but rather on a sliding scale. This sliding scale resembles a seesaw more so than a definitive *healthy* or *unhealthy*. On this metaphorical seesaw, your health may tip from one end to the other, between healthy and unhealthy for certain markers of health. However, this does not make you healthy or unhealthy in an absolute sense. Even when you experience signs of ill-health, such as pain, infection, inflammation, poor sleep or low mood, you may still be considered generally *healthy* when considering the wide spectrum of health markers. This is because health is not static… it is dynamic.

On top of this, no markers of health can guarantee your future health. Yes, there are guidelines to prevent or treat illness or disease; however, there are no guarantees that taking certain actions will prevent or reverse disease or ill health. For instance, despite the convincing statistics that alcohol, smoking, trans fats, added salt, added sugar and processed meats contribute to poor health, these behaviours in no way lead to definite poor health. You've probably heard of someone who did everything *right* for their health yet developed cancer.

On the flip side, you may have heard of a long-lived person who smoked and ate a seemingly unhealthy diet their entire life. The thing is, no lifestyle program, superfood, supplement or exercise regime can guarantee optimal health or even the prevention of disease and illness.

Furthermore, there are no lifestyle changes you can adopt that will prevent you from dying, as you will do so eventually. Other life events that are completely out of your control may lead to your demise or impact your health in unintentional ways. Thus, there is some truth to the common justification for unhealthy eating that some people use, when they say for example, 'one doughnut is not going to kill me'. One doughnut is not going to sabotage your weight or health, let alone kill you. Even if you consumed a dozen doughnuts tomorrow, you are unlikely to keel over and die. Eating doughnuts habitually every day may have long-term health consequences, yet there is still no absolute guarantee it will. Any speculation on health risk is based on population-level data and does not account for your unique genetic predisposition and complete lifestyle.

Now, I'm not suggesting that you eat copious doughnuts or that you shouldn't adopt healthy lifestyle behaviours. What I'm suggesting is that rather than seeing markers of health as a predictor of your fate, or feeling like a victim to your diagnosis or body, use these markers of health (and associated guidelines) as signposts to prioritise healthy behaviour changes. In this way, you can take action in a more relaxed way without the *must-achieve* mentality that does more to perpetuate stress, guilt and shame, than to promote self-care.

Trending diets and health claims for supplements or alternative therapies frequently prey on the fear of illness and death. There is nothing wrong with eating wholefoods, taking nutritional supplements (if the diet is inadequate or deficiencies are detected), having a massage for muscle tension or meditating to reduce stress. These can be incredibly beneficial practices in maintaining good health: physically, mentally and emotionally. However, it can be an issue when the main motivator to adopt healthful behaviours is fear.

In a state of fear, you might place an immense expectation on your eating and lifestyle behaviours, possibly becoming inflexible in your approach, and eroding the very health benefits you aspire to attain. Healthy eating can become unhealthy when you spend a considerable portion of your day thinking about, choosing and preparing healthy food, so that it interferes with other activities in your life. Or when you allow the fear of being overweight, unhealthy or dying, prevent you from living your life to the fullest.

Psychologists now recognise an obsession with healthy eating as a concern. Orthorexia, although not yet recognised as a clinically diagnosable eating disorder, occurs when an individual becomes obsessed with healthy eating so much so that it impacts their life (43,44). It doesn't refer to an individual who enjoys a visit to the farmers' market and makes their own sauerkraut. Rather it refers to an individual who partakes in similar activities to the point that they're paranoid about food. They may disengage in social activities for fear of the possible food served and feel anxious about shopping, preparing food and eating.

If Not Dieting, Then What?

You may now be wondering, since dieting and aspiring for optimal health does not ensure your well-being, whether you should release the reins of control and give up on being healthy. Not exactly: you can loosen the reins of control without it being an act of giving up or giving in. I believe that you can nourish and nurture your body without the need for deprivation, restriction, control, guilt or shame. Further, I believe that the pursuit of a certain weight, body shape or health goals can be the very preoccupation that starves you of the happiness and contentment in your body and yourself that you seek. Allow me to explain why in the next chapter.

Joyful Eating Principle 1.
ABANDON DIETING

You are not a failure for being unable to achieve or maintain results with a diet. Diets fail you because they promote immense hunger, slow your metabolism, and perpetuate yo-yo dieting, weight cycling, body dissatisfaction and distrust in your body. Moreover, they provide no guarantee of good health or happiness. Ditch the diet mentality and step off the diet cycle, to foster a healthier relationship with food and your body.

3

Are You Starving Yourself of Happiness?

"It is not uncommon for people to spend their whole life waiting to start living."

— Eckhart Tolle, *The Power of Now: A Guide to Spiritual Enlightenment*

Whether you desire weight loss to get back into those skinny jeans or for health reasons, continually striving for these types of goals can keep you trapped in the diet cycle. You could say that it starves you of happiness. Before exploring why this may be, I encourage you to reflect on your weight loss and health goals.

> ### ✍ Journal your weight loss and health goals
>
> Take a moment to consider your weight loss or health goals up to this point in time, and record them in your Workbook or journal. If they've changed since beginning this book, note how they have changed.

It's commonly believed that you need to set goals in order to take action as well as stay motivated to create change in your life. However, a focus on goal setting may not be as effective as you've been led to believe. Goal setting may actually sabotage your efforts. Let me explain.

The Fundamental Flaw of Goal Setting

It's a common belief that if you were to draw a straight line from where you are to where you want to be—your desired weight or health goals—this line would be either straight or possibly step-like. Unfortunately, however, you're unlikely to experience the journey from where you are now to your intended goal in this linear or stepwise fashion, but rather experience it with many ups and downs, unexpected twists and turns.

At times you may feel like your goals are too far away, that the progress you're making is too slow or insubstantial, or even that you're completely off track. The journey towards your goals might not resemble a straight line or steps, but may appear more like that of a lost, neurotic snail that loops back over its intended path, time and time again. Subsequently, you may feel like you've *lost your way* or that you've no hope of reaching your intended goal.

So, why is this so common? An issue with goal setting is that it draws your attention to the two ends of the journey: at one end is where you've come from and what you no longer want, and at the other, where you want to go and what you want to achieve. Unfortunately, however, placing your attention on either end of this journey can sabotage your efforts. This is because it can intensify the importance of achieving your goals and lead you to push and force yourself, adopting extreme and unsustainable behaviours.

This focus on what you want to achieve can cause you to take various actions that you don't enjoy. So it is the destination, not the journey you are prioritising; contrary to the saying, *life is a journey, not a destination.*

Further, the false perception that everything will change—for the better—when you reach your final destination can cause you to place great expectation and attachment to achieving the end goal. This in turn can amplify success or failure.

Self-help gurus and life coaches may chant, 'fail to plan, plan to fail'. However, a plan is only your best guess (or your health practitioner's or online health guru's). Life happens, other priorities come up, and you don't have absolute control over whether life unfolds according to your plans. As John Lennon said, 'life is what happens to you while you're busy making other plans'.

When you go on a diet, you do so with expectations, realistic or unrealistic, that you'll achieve certain results. If you've read a diet book or seen a weight loss consultant, you may have been promised certain outcomes, such as a weight loss range to expect each week or by the end of the program. However, when you have an expectation, it's hard *not* to think about it each day, or even multiple times a day. You'll be tempted to hop on the scales or look in the mirror and contemplate whether you've made progress and are on course to achieve the outcome you want by your imagined deadline.

During this time, day-by-day or week-by-week, if you don't see the results you're expecting you can easily feel disheartened. As a consequence, you may push harder, possibly employing the fitness mantra 'no pain, no gain'. You may deprive yourself further or even more diligently follow the diet or exercise plan. Alternatively, you may think, *why bother, who was I kidding anyway, I'm not going to be able to shift this weight!*

More specifically, if you don't achieve the results you desire on a diet, you may think one of three things:

1. *This approach to weight loss has failed me; I need to find another approach.* This thinking can cause you to swap and change your approach, continually searching for the *miracle* weight loss diet, and subsequently, never fully commit to a way of eating or habits that nourish and support your body.
2. *I have failed.* This thinking may cause you to believe you need to be more disciplined to achieve your goals. You may restrict or deprive yourself further. You carry on, committing more money to diet programs and products, or looking for someone to be accountable to in the hope that this will keep you on track to achieve your desired results. Believing you have failed at dieting can lead to immense guilt.

3. *I am a complete failure; my body is either broken or I don't have what it takes to lose weight.* This thinking is the consequence of attaching your self-worth and identity to your body and to your ability to achieve your goals. It can cause you to adopt behaviours that are disrespectful of your body or self-harming. You may give up all attempts to achieve your weight and health goals. Believing you are a failure can lead to immense shame.

The thing is, you have not failed diets, diets have failed you. None of the above thoughts and subsequent actions promote self-care. Rather, they lead you to fight against your body and perpetuate dissatisfaction and self-loathing, which do more to sabotage your efforts.

Furthermore, it is likely that what you truly desire is not the end goal or weight loss per se, but what you believe it will enable you to do. And quite possibly, it's what your weight, size or body shape says about who you are as a person. Let's explore this further.

✍ What have you been holding off?

Reflect on what actions and emotional states you've made dependent on achieving your desired weight or size. Consider:

- appearance and clothing
- eating and food choices
- relationships
- social life
- movement and exercise
- sexuality
- travel, and
- career.

Record a statement about your desired weight or size as identified in the previous Self-Reflection Activity in your Workbook or journal and then list what you believe this will enable you to do or feel. For example, you may record a statement such as, *when I am so and so kilograms, I will…*, or *when I drop back to such and such dress size, I will…*

- *stop incessantly thinking about what I eat*
- *have more time for my partner, kids or work*
- *feel content with my body*
- *feel good about how I look*
- *feel comfortable in a bikini*
- *stop wearing frumpy clothing*
- *wear or purchase some nice underwear*
- *be more confident*
- *get a fun new haircut*
- *have family photos taken*
- *be able to buy stunning clothing*
- *feel sexy and desirable to my partner*
- *be able to start dating*
- *attract an intimate partner*

cont.

- *be able to leave my partner*
- *feel comfortable to be naked*
- *be able to enjoy the beach and swimming*
- *feel worthy of love and success*
- *be more adventurous (e.g. surfing, bike riding)*
- *be able to go on holiday*
- *go out dancing*
- *be a better example for my kids*
- *have more energy to have fun*
- *be able to accept myself for who I am*
- *be more confident to approach my boss about a pay raise*
- *get a new job*
- *no longer be self-conscious when I have to tuck my shirt into my pants*
- *be able to join a gym*

Once you've created your list, reflect on whether there is a true physical restriction due to your weight or size, or whether these are conditions your mind has created that prevent you from doing these things right now. Look at your list and ask yourself: *Is it true that I can't do this till I lose weight? Am I holding myself back from embracing and boldly enjoying life? Why?*

You may like to set yourself a challenge to do something on your list. Doing or attempting to do something you'd previously thought conditional on your weight and size can shed light on your true fears and doubts. Record how this challenge makes you feel and the thoughts that arise in your Workbook or journal.

The basis of goal setting is to motivate yourself through the identification of both what you do not want and what you want to achieve. It is founded on thinking and believing: *I'll be happy when...*

So, you may think: *I'll be happy when I reach my ideal weight. I'll be happy when I lose 10 kg. I'll be happy when I am a size 12. I'll be happy when I can fit into my old jeans. I'll be happy when I can control my eating habits. I'll be happy when I get my dream job. I'll be happy when I enter a loving relationship.*

Ultimately, however, what you want is not simply to be able to buy stunning clothes, enjoy swimming, start dating, go out dancing or even gain more confidence. Deep down what you really want is how you believe these things will make you feel: happy, content, enough and lovable.

Unfortunately, despite what you've been led to believe by life coaches and self-help books, achieving goals is not a guarantee of anyone's happiness. You cannot know with absolute certainty that achieving your goals will ensure your happiness and end the self-doubt and lack of confidence you may feel. You don't know whether achieving your goals will be everything you imagined and more, or whether it will be a complete letdown.

The expectation that you will feel happy and content when you achieve your goals is only a story your mind makes up to keep you striving. So often, and you may have experienced this yourself, you might achieve a goal and immediately start striving for the next. It may have been that achieving your goal was not what you expected, or perhaps you still didn't feel you were good enough. As a consequence, you may find yourself shifting the goalpost: *if I just lose these last few kilos, then I'll be happy.*

Continually striving to do better and be better is socially revered. At a young age, society reinforces that you should keep striving to do better, with comments such as: 'wow, look at what you created, imagine what you could achieve if you put more effort in'; or, 'great win on the field today, you have a great future ahead of you in the big leagues'.

As a consequence of the constantly moving goal posts, you can feel like you never get *there*. Furthermore, even if you achieve your goals and they're exactly what you dreamt, you can end up living with the constant fear of losing these achievements. Alternatively, you might feel the pressure of maintaining your accomplishments or status.

The consequence of single-mindedly focusing on achieving your goals is that rather than fully enjoying your successes, you're likely to apply more pressure on yourself to keep achieving. You are unlikely to enjoy each step as your focus is on the contribution toward achieving your end goal.

Don't get me wrong; there is nothing wrong with committing to a passion, showing up to train, or perfecting your craft or vocation. The issue is that you can spend a lot of your life pushing yourself through a process that you don't enjoy in order to achieve an end goal, only to turn around and begin striving for the next or become immediately dissatisfied.

The fundamental flaw of goal setting is believing that you acquire happiness and contentment through an external source or achievement. However, nothing, absolutely nothing, needs to change for you to embrace happiness in this moment. Happiness is not something you acquire or deserve. You can spend your entire life chasing goals, essentially robbing yourself of happiness and contentment right now. However, your level of happiness and contentment are the result of how you perceive the world and your internal state of being, not what you achieve.

It's not an easy concept to integrate. You may feel resistance to prioritising happiness and contentment over attaining your goals, as perhaps you fear you'd no longer *strive* to improve your health or take action. Yet the opposite is more likely true. Shifting your focus to feeling happy and content right now can enable you to nurture yourself in a way that makes you feel good—happy, content, energetic and alive—rather than push and punish yourself to achieve.

You may also fear that if you shift your focus to feeling good, you won't be able to control yourself around food. However, if you do crave certain foods and eat compulsively, it's unlikely because they make you *feel good*. The uncontrollable cravings and eating behaviour are more likely the result of restriction and deprivation. When you no longer use food as a reward, a punishment or as a way to numb out, you're more likely to find yourself making food choices to nourish your body. More on this later.

Diets Cultivate a Resistance to Change

> *"Shame corrodes that very part of us that*
> *believes we are capable of change."*

—Brené Brown, *I Thought It Was Just Me (But It Isn't)*

Consciously, you may have an immense desire to achieve your weight loss or health goals and can't comprehend why you may sabotage your efforts. I've discovered that conflicting goals, values and fears are common barriers to people's attempts to lose weight and improve their health. Let me share three client cases to explain:

1. A lady in her late forties desired to lose weight to attract a partner but sabotaged her healthy eating efforts whenever she was lonely, binging on foods that she perceived as unhealthy. Through exploring her conflicting goals and fears, we discovered that she not only feared being alone, she also feared having her heart broken, again. Although she wanted an intimate relationship, she was afraid to enter into one. And although she wanted to lose weight—thinking that this is what would attract a partner—she was afraid to lose weight.

    The thing is, she could not know for certain that she couldn't find a partner at her current weight, or whether her next relationship would end in heartbreak. What she was afraid of was the unknown—what might or might not eventuate—and was completely unrelated to how much she weighed. It was only her mind that had made an association between weight, love and intimacy. It became clear that associating weight loss with attracting a partner was sabotaging her efforts to adopt healthier lifestyle behaviours.

2. A lady in her early forties, although concerned about the health consequences of her weight, was conflicted about pursuing weight loss as she was a feminist. She didn't want others to think she was merely adopting exercise and eating healthily to be attractive to the opposite sex. She wanted recognition for her intellect, not her body.

However, being beautiful doesn't mean you can't be intelligent, and you can be a champion for women's rights no matter how you look. Objectification of one's body and assumptions of who you are based on how you look, will unfortunately always occur. You cannot control how others perceive you by your physicality or apparent intellect.

Through this understanding, she could begin to see that the only person's perception of her body that could hurt her was her own. It was her perception of her body and how it should or should not look based on her values, which prevented her from moving and nourishing her body in ways that supported it.

3. A lady in her early fifties had been overweight since her late twenties. She came to see me as she wanted to lose weight due to health concerns and a desire to travel. She recalled that when she was in her twenties her friends were jealous of her good looks and ability to joke around with the guys. They feared that she'd *steal* their boyfriends. Thus, they would exclude her from certain gatherings.

   Now, years later, she feared that if she lost her weight, her friends would be threatened by her again. However, being beautiful doesn't mean you are a cheater or that you would reciprocate advances. The insecurity her friends felt originated from their fears and actually had nothing to do with her. Yes, it can hurt when your friends or others think negatively about you, but how others think is not within your control. Sabotaging your health and contentment does not serve anyone, especially not you.

I hope these examples demonstrate how much more there is to your desire to change. Let's identify your conflicting goals, desires and values with regards to your weight loss or health goals.

✍ Why you may embrace or resist change?

To understand why and how you might sabotage your efforts, it can be useful to complete a behaviour change matrix, where you ask yourself the following questions in turn:

i.   Benefits of staying the same?

ii. Concerns with staying the same?

iii. Concerns about change?

iv. Reasons to change?

These questions are presented in a table (see below), to enable you to compare your responses side by side. You can complete this table in your Workbook or draw up the table in your journal. Then ask yourself each question in turn, writing down everything that comes to mind without censoring or judging what you write. Be as thorough as possible.

i. Benefits of staying the same? (e.g. staying your current weight)	iii. Reasons to change? (e.g. reasons to lose weight)
ii. Concerns with staying the same? (e.g. remaining your current weight)	iv. Concerns about change? (e.g. concerns or fear of losing weight)

Below I've provided example responses to each of the questions, which may help stimulate thoughts that you might not have previously considered.

cont.

i. Benefits of staying the same?

Contrary to what you may believe, it is possible that you fear you will achieve your desired goals, as there may be some benefits of not changing, such as:

- *I won't feel deprived of my favourite foods*
- *I won't have to monitor what I eat constantly*
- *I won't have to maintain control of my eating*
- *I won't have to purchase an entirely new wardrobe of clothing*
- *I won't be a threat to my married friends*
- *I'll be able to continue going unnoticed*

Some of the thoughts that come to mind may seem superficial or superfluous. Write them down anyway, as they take up space in your mind.

ii. Concerns with staying the same?

Your concerns with staying the same represent the dissatisfaction and discontentment that often motivates change. These could be:

- *I'll increase my chance of obesity-related health conditions*
- *I'll remain unattractive and unlovable*
- *I won't be a good role model for my children*
- *I will continue to be judged by my mother, friends or complete strangers*
- *I will continue to be invisible to others, like I don't matter*

iii. Concerns about change?

Concerns about change are the fears that arise when you think of making a change, or in the case of weight loss, the fears associated with losing weight. Concerns for change could be:

- *It will be hard work*
- *It will result in hard work for the rest of my life to maintain the weight loss*

cont.

- *I won't be able to enjoy indulgent treats*
- *I'll be missing out on one of life's pleasures—food*
- *I'll have to consider everything I ever eat*
- *I'll have less time for other activities I enjoy, as I have to commit to exercise*
- *I won't be able to enjoy social gatherings with my friends and family*
- *I'll need to be considerably more prepared and organised*
- *I'll need to consistently and persistently deprive myself*
- *I'll be noticed and have to show the world who I really am*
- *I'll have nothing else to fix*
- *I'll have to embrace life and stop holding back*
- *I won't have my weight to blame for my perceived shortfalls*
- *I'll fear putting the weight back on*
- *I might look older or unattractive with saggy, excess skin*
- *I'll be admired just for the way I look, not my intellect*
- *I'd draw attention to myself, and I'm not ready to get intimate with anyone*
- *People might think that I'm shallow and that I value appearance above all else*
- *I may become romantically involved, and fear:*
  - *I'll lose my independence*
  - *I'll have my heart broken, again*
  - *I'll lose my single friends due to jealousy*
  - *I'll have to maintain the weight loss to keep my partner, or*
  - *that a pregnancy could cause me to put the weight back on (if my new partner wants to start a family) and he'll leave me*

iv. Reasons to change?

The reasons to change are often what you perceive as the benefits of change, and thus your motivators to change. Reasons to change regarding your weight and health could be:

- *I'll be able to wear the beautiful clothing I used to wear*
- *My legs will no longer chaff*

cont.

44

- *I'll be able to exercise without pain in my knees*
- *My husband will become more interested in me sexually*
- *I'll be able to travel without taking up two seats on the plane*
- *I'll be able to attend a yoga class without feeling conspicuous*
- *I'll enjoy better health*
- *I'll have more energy to do the things I want in life*
- *I'll be able to reveal the real me*
- *People will stop staring at me at restaurants, whether I order a salad or burger and fries*

Hopefully, you'll now be more aware of the thoughts and barriers you have about your weight and weight loss. Some of your responses for the *Benefits-of* and *Concerns with staying the same* may be real barriers, such as a physical impediment. Others may be perceived: they are barriers your mind has constructed.

For example, resistance to doing a yoga class may be due to pain in your knees, which is a true physical impediment. However, who says that you need to do yoga to be healthy? There are countless alternative forms of exercise you could try. There are also modifications that can be made in a yoga class with the guidance of a considerate and attentive instructor. Despite having a physical impediment, it's your mind that has attached conditions of what you can and can't do as a consequence. It's these thoughts, rather than the pain in your knees, which prevents you from embracing any form of exercise.

On the other hand, feeling conspicuous in a yoga class is a restriction constructed entirely by your mind. It is likely to stem from a fear of judgement or of not being good enough. I'm not suggesting you *feel the fear and do it anyway*, but explore your beliefs and the rules you've imposed on yourself, which you'll have the opportunity to do later.

Diets Require Unsustainable Motivation

The thought of changing your body and your life can be exhilarating. Like many others, you may have experienced the excitement of going on a new diet or lifestyle program. You may have purchased books, workout clothing or equipment. You may have plastered images of a slimmer you or someone you aspire to look like on a vision board. You may have filled your fridge with foods prescribed on a meal plan.

However, like the vast majority of people, you may have found that the exhilaration wanes as the road ahead begins to feel daunting and unattainable. It could be that you don't see results fast enough, or as depicted in the diet program you're following. You may have challenges or other priorities come up in your life. You might even feel emotionally drained by life circumstances. Whatever the case, it is completely normal to find that you don't have the motivation to continue.

When motivation wanes, you may believe that the negatives of staying the same were not substantial enough to keep you driven. But is that true?

Life coaches and motivational speakers often exaggerate the consequences of staying the same and the benefits of succeeding in order to generate a greater drive to achieve goals. Some believe that an awareness of the *worst-case* or *doomsday* scenario will keep you motivated.

A devastating health prognosis may well motivate you to action, but this action may be in a state of panic. Thus, the change created in your lifestyle may be drastic and unsustainable. You may be able to keep it up for a while. However, to stay motivated you'll have to remind yourself of the negative consequences of not taking action, or how you don't want to be where you are right now, for example, that you don't want to be a diabetic or have heart disease.

Motivation in this way can backfire. A devastating health prognosis can immobilise you as you find yourself in a state of disbelief or uncertainty. You might think: *I can't do anything, it's too late, it's genetics anyway,* or *I'll die of something, why fight it?*

46

Consequently, you might not take action to help yourself. Perhaps you passively allow medical professionals to take over the reins of your body's health, without an understanding or awareness of your health issues. Trusting in the abilities of your medical team is important in your healing and recovery. Yet when it's done in a defeatist way, it can be disempowering and perpetuate inaction. The thing is, I don't believe that it is motivation you require to create change. Let me explain why.

Motivation requires sufficient discontentment with your current situation that you are moved to take steps to change. However, it is this dissatisfaction and discontentment that can sabotage your efforts. Firstly, it may sabotage your efforts because it can lead you to adopt unsustainable actions out of fear of staying the same. Secondly, even if you change your body, the self-deprecating internal dialogue may persist. Achieving your goals is not a sure-fire way to your happiness nor a way to quieten your *inner critic.*

Whether your body changes or not, if your inner critic causes you to feel that you're not worthy of success or happiness, it will continue to either sabotage your efforts or prevent you from ever feeling truly happy. Your inner critic can, therefore, keep you trapped in procrastination, second-guessing yourself, giving up at the first sign of failure and sabotaging your efforts in a myriad of ways. It is your inner critic that whispers, or in some cases, screams at you: *who were you kidding; you don't have what it takes; you're never going to be acceptable; you'll end up putting it back on anyway.* Even if you achieve your initial desired goals, you may still not feel confident or good enough to pursue bigger dreams and passions, because your inner critic continues to *tell* you that you aren't worthy of success. It is more likely that it is your inner critic that's holding you back from living your life to the fullest, not your weight.

Although I encourage you to let go of motivating yourself through dissatisfaction and discontentment, I'm not suggesting that you take no action. Instead, I recommend that you create change from a place of inspiration, rather than motivation. You may wonder how motivation and inspiration differ.

Motivation originates from external factors that push you to take action to control or force an outcome: to move from what you don't want to what you want. Motivation is logical and calculated. Conversely, inspiration occurs as internal momentum that compels you to take action—like drawing a moth to a flame. Inspiration can feel like a gut reaction or a heart's desire.

Inspiration plants the seed of an idea, yet it is not required each day to take action. Action, instead, requires that you *show up* to enable inspiration to flow through you. Invoking this state involves commitment and persistence without an attachment to the end goal. It involves switching your focus to how the action makes you *feel* in each step and then reminding yourself of this feeling so as to stay committed. For example, you may love the feeling in your body after completing a yoga class, and it is this feeling more so than the yoga class itself which keeps you showing up to class.

Inspiration arises when instead of forcing and controlling, you are relaxed, and your mind is quiet—enabling you to *listen* to your gut or heart. Later I'll share how you can foster this deep sense of relaxation and quieten your inner critic to allow inspiration to come through. For now, I hope you can see how your inner critic squashes inspiration, by perpetuating self-doubt and causing you to push yourself in an unsustainable way.

Diets Stimulate Procrastination: the Diet Starts Tomorrow

Despite your desire to attain your goals, you may have experienced times when you do not take the necessary action. You may have found yourself wondering: *why am I not jumping out of bed to put on my running shoes? Why am I checking my Facebook feed when I really should be preparing a healthy meal? Why am I hitting snooze on the alarm and instead of eating breakfast at home as planned, grabbing a coffee and snack to go?* These are all signs of procrastination, which is the consequence of resistance to start or undertake the action required to *achieve* a desired goal or outcome.

In procrastination, you may say to yourself: *I'll start when... I'll start when the kids go back to school. I'll start eating healthier when I've finished the kitchen renovations or purchased a juicer. I'll prioritise eating healthier after this deadline at work.*

However, distractions and challenges like these will always come up in life and there is never going to be a *perfect time* to start. You'll always be able to find a reason to say, *I'll start when…*

Procrastination might be a consequence of fear of the hard work required to attain your goals. It may be that you're uncertain or doubt whether you'll succeed: *Will it work? Can I do it? Do I have what it takes? Have I selected the right diet to lose weight or cure my irritable bowel syndrome?*

Procrastination might occur because you fear failure or success. You may fear the loss of self-identity if you succeed in making a change. You may fear the ever-expanding goals and expectations that snowball from the goals you set yourself.

Procrastination might also present itself as perfectionism. Perfectionism can result in inaction unless the plan is *perfect*. It can cause you to give up unless you can get it *right*. Perfectionism can cause you to second-guess your approach or switch tactics continually so that you never really commit to an action. Perfectionism can prevent you from finishing tasks or attaining your goals, as your perception is: *not attempted is better than failed or less than perfect.*

However, perfection is only an illusion your mind makes up: there is no absolute right or wrong approach to health. Aspiring for perfection only serves to prevent you from making progress in adopting healthy lifestyle behaviours. Unlike the prevailing saying, 'good is the enemy of great', I favour what author Elizabeth Gilbert's mother used to say to her as a child that she carried through to complete her award-winning books, 'done is better than good'.

Diets Perpetuate Fear

Fear frequently underlies the internal conflict to work towards your goals. It is fear that can cause you to act, and it is fear that can hold you back.

If you reexamine your responses in the Self-Reflection Activity: *Why you may embrace or resist change?,* you may be able to identify the underlying fears. You may then notice that you fear:

- the consequences of staying your current weight
- the hard work of losing weight and maintaining weight loss
- the changes you have made conditional on weight loss
- how others perceive you, at any weight
- what sort of person you will become or have to be once you lose weight
- not being lovable or acceptable, even once you lose weight
- becoming unwell and not being able to enjoy your life fully
- dying alone, or in a long-drawn-out, painful way, without your full physical and mental capacities

You are certainly not alone in your fears. It's common to fear not being enough, not being lovable, safe, secure; to fear judgement, ridicule, failure; and to fear pain, suffering, dying or dying alone.

Achieving your goals is unlikely to resolve these fears, and at the same time you're more likely to keep striving for goal after goal, looking for that which could provide you with a deep sense of happiness and contentment. However, achieving your goals provides no guarantee of happiness. There will always be more for you to achieve or perfect to feel worthy.

The thing is, you can experience happiness right now, without changing a thing. You can do this by learning to quieten your internal, self-critical voice that sabotages you and promotes fear. You may still set yourself challenges and choose to adopt healthier lifestyle behaviours, however, you can do so without attaching your self-worth or identity to your ability to achieve. It is this attachment that causes you to place immense pressure on yourself and so does not serve you to nourish and care for your body.

Let's put an end to starving yourself of happiness to achieve your goals... and release the weight of dieting.

4

Free Yourself of Diet Stress

"For some reason, we are truly convinced that if we criticize ourselves, the criticism will lead to change. If we are harsh, we believe we will end up being kind. If we shame ourselves, we believe we end up loving ourselves. It has never been true, not for a moment, that shame leads to love. Only love leads to love."

— Geneen Roth

Your body interprets dieting as stress, both physically and mentally. It doesn't know the difference between a famine, where you have to be alert and on the ready to acquire food, and a self-induced calorie restriction. In this chapter, I explain how stress can sabotage your weight and health, and share ways to mitigate the adverse consequences of stress.

The Stress Response

When you experience stress, there is a physiological response in your body, known as the *stress* or *fight-or-flight response*. The hypothalamus, a gland in the brain, controls the stress response. It activates the sympathetic nervous system, which regulates automatic bodily functions that enable you to either run from danger or swiftly deal with threatening situations.

Some of the physiological responses activated in the stress response include:

- increased blood sugar (glucose)
- increased insulin (regulation of blood sugar)
- increased heart rate and blood pressure
- slowed metabolism
- increased cortisol
- altered levels of other hormones (incl. those that regulate hunger and satiety)
- reduced blood flow to the digestive system (45)

These physiological responses can all contribute to decreased weight loss when you restrict calories or deprive yourself of foods. They can also cause accelerated weight gain when you resume your *normal* intake, that is, once you quit a diet (37). Furthermore, increased cortisol can increase stress-induced overeating and promote fat storage and insulin resistance (46,47).

An added implication of the stress response is that the body diverts blood away from the digestive system, as it is a less vital function for immediate survival than the muscles and heart, which enable you to jolt into immediate action. Therefore, the stress response influences appetite, hunger and satiation signals between the brain and gut (48). Stress can impact how effectively your body assimilates nutrients, and how it responds to the foods you consume.

The link between stress and physiological factors is the consequence of brain-gut interactions, commonly termed the *brain-gut axis* (48). This axis is the connection between the neural network in the brain and the gut.

Research has found that stress contributes to digestive disturbance and alterations in gut health, such as:

- Irritable bowel syndrome (IBS)
- Inflammatory bowel disease (IBD)

- Gastroesophageal reflux disease (GERD)
- Peptic ulcer
- immune response to foods
- altered gastrointestinal motility
- increased visceral perception (sensations originating from the gut)
- changed gastrointestinal secretions
- increased intestinal permeability
- negative effects on the regenerative capacity of gastrointestinal mucosa and mucosal blood flow
- negative effects on intestinal microbiota (48,49,50)

Therefore, improving or resolving such issues requires consideration not only of what you eat but of your stress load. Furthermore, stress can also impact your relationship with food by influencing what you choose to eat and your eating behaviour.

Stress Affects Your Food Choices and Eating Behaviour

How your body responds to stress differs with intensity and type of stress. It also differs between people. Under stress, some people may feel a suppression of their appetite and don't feel like eating at all. Others may feel hungry, but can't seem to eat enough to satisfy their appetite; they can eat and eat without filling the empty feeling.

Scientific research supports that stress can either increase or decrease caloric intake. Chronic stress can promote either obesity or anorexia, depending on the individual and dietary environments (48,51).

There appears to be an interplay between physiological and psychological causes of food choices when stressed, which can potentially increase your likelihood of selecting sweet, fatty and energy-dense foods (38,52). Despite a physiological demand for sweet and fatty foods, it is the psychological association that creates appeal for certain foods when stressed. Therefore, although fruit and nuts are sweet and fatty, they are generally not the foods you reach for when stressed; rather it is foods that are perceived as *treat foods*, such as pizza, cookies and chocolate.

While most treat foods are far more intensely sweet and fatty than fruit and nuts, and this does play a role in the preference for them when stressed, equally influential are the labels assigned to these foods. It is the perception of foods as a *treat* that increases preference and perceived liking of these foods, and can result in an increased likelihood of you eating them when you're stressed (40).

Furthermore, the preference for treat foods is intensified by dieting. A study of work stress demonstrated that the food intake of dieters (termed 'restrained eaters' in the study) was influenced by stress more so than unrestrained eaters. Stress resulted in higher energy, saturated fat and sugar intake in restrained than unrestrained eaters (53).

I'm not suggesting that you never eat when you feel stressed. Sometimes you have to eat under stress because you require the fuel to have the mental and physical energy for the activities in your day. In some instances, eating in response to stress may be the healthiest option. Eating is considerably healthier and safer than, say, drugs, excessive alcohol, unsafe sex or self-harm to cope with stress. Eating may have been, or may continue to be, a crucial coping mechanism for you to deal with stress and emotional distress from time to time, and that's perfectly acceptable.

Furthermore, ascribing to the rule to *not* eat unhealthy food when you're stressed can actually compound the stress. Resisting the use of food to soothe stress can do more to perpetuate feelings of guilt and shame than it does to enable you to work through your feelings or deal with life circumstances.

Therefore, rather than ceasing all stress-induced eating, I encourage you to explore your triggers for stress and associated eating with curiosity. You might embrace other activities to de-stress rather than eat. However, do so only when it occurs to you and feels like the most self-nurturing thing to do in the moment.

Perpetrators of Stress

Although stress initiates physiological and psychological responses, it's more a consequence of how you interpret the world around you, rather than what's going on in your life. Deadlines, trauma, loss, expectations, discrimination and socioeconomic factors all play a role in stress, yet each person will perceive them differently. Thus, the intensity of stress you experience is the result of how you perceive your reality. Stress response is manifested through the thoughts and beliefs associated with what's happening in your life.

Feeling stress is the result of your thoughts about what should or should not have happened in the past, and the future consequences and implications of your actions. Stress arises when you're caught up in wanting to change what has already occurred, or thinking that you can control your behaviour or similar events in the future.

Unfortunately, your brain doesn't know the difference between reality—what is truly occurring in the world around you—and the stories your mind makes up. Nor does your body distinguish between true danger and your thoughts. As a consequence, your thoughts of the past or future can influence the physical sensations in your body in this moment, as if the events were occurring right now.

Let Go of Diet Stress

The belief that you can control your weight and health can provoke stress that may be further amplified if you can't lose weight, you regain weight or become ill. Reprimanding yourself for failing at a diet, or raiding the pantry when worried, can stimulate the stress response in your body. Reprimands do more to stimulate stress-induced eating than they do to promote a healthy relationship with food. Further, the confusing and conflicting information on what you *should* or *should not* eat may be an additional stressor.

If you feel resistance to letting go of the stress of dieting, you are not alone. It's a widely-held belief that the stress of dieting has got to be better than being overweight. However, research indicates that reducing stress may have the most profound effect on your health, even when you consider conditions such as diabetes, atherosclerosis, cardiovascular disease and metabolic disorders, which are frequently correlated to weight (37,46).

Further, if you believe that what you're eating contributes to good health, more likely than not it will. Remarkably, research has demonstrated that the way you think about food, your health prognosis or treatments, can alter their effectiveness. This is likely to be the result of the placebo effect, which occurs when you believe something is going to do you good or have a specific effect on your body, and consequently it does, even if you are given a *sham* medication or treatment, such as a sugar pill (54). Consistent with this, a study found that beliefs about the energy content of foods may exert stronger effects on hunger than their true energy value (55).

Now, I'm not suggesting that you can eat anything and believing it will do your body good, will make it so. However, eating in a relaxed state, without the self-deprecating self-talk, may potentially contribute to your body responding positively to the nourishment you provide it.

Deactivate the Stress Response

Adopting some simple practices to deactivate the stress response can serve to reduce not only the consequences of stress but also the occurrence of stress-induced and emotional eating. There are many ways you can reduce stress and initiate what is known as the *relaxation response*, such as taking time out for yourself, engaging in flow activities, or other relaxation techniques. Let's begin with taking some time out for yourself with what I like to term *me time*.

✍ Carve out me time

Taking time out for yourself can promote good mental health and reduce the physiological and psychological responses to stress. Consider what *me time* activities you enjoy that relax and re-energise you. Record these activities as a list in your Workbook or journal. Examples include:

- listening to, singing along with, or dancing to music while doing nothing else, especially not chores
- drinking a cup of tea or coffee in a relaxing environment, such as a café or outdoors
- taking a gentle walk in a beautiful or peaceful area
- having a bath
- getting a massage
- taking a nap
- reading an enjoyable book
- visiting a library or art gallery
- cooking a delicious meal
- lying in the sun with your eyes closed for 5-10 minutes
- enjoying a beautiful view or time out in nature
- lighting a candle or diffusing essential oils when you arrive home
- journaling your feelings
- drawing or doodling for relaxation
- meditating or other relaxation tools
- deep breathing

Once you've compiled a list of *me time* activities, consider which activity you'd like to adopt first and schedule it into your day or week. The activity you choose doesn't need to take a considerable amount of time; it may just be five to fifteen minutes of reading a book or doodling in a journal.

Recognising Resistance to Taking 'Me Time'

It's important that your *me time* activities don't become another chore or something you feel like you've failed at if you don't get around to doing it. The purpose is solely to bring you joy and relaxation. If you frequently talk yourself out of taking *me time* or just allow life to get in the way, try to remember the feeling of anxiety and tension when you don't give yourself this *me time*.

You may notice some resistance to taking up yet another activity in your day or week. It's all too easy to fill a *spare* ten minutes with a *to-do* task or to prioritise other people's needs above your own self-care. It's possible that you feel guilty or self-indulgent for doing so. However, taking time for yourself may enable you to provide more focused and dedicated attention when you do undertake your tasks and responsibilities. Although this may be the case, the purpose is to fulfil your own needs, rather than the needs of others. It is just that this may be a flow-on consequence.

You may want to consider forming a ritual to establish your *me time* activity. Psychologists suggest that it can be helpful to attach new activities that you want to form into a habit to other activities you do every day, such as showering, arriving home from work, or putting the children to bed.

If you feel too tired to take some time out for yourself, be aware that obtaining adequate and refreshing sleep is important in reducing the stress response. Sleep has the potential to influence your subsequent food choices, your hunger and metabolism. Sleep-deprived individuals are more likely to choose less healthful foods, prefer caloric dense foods, snack more frequently and have more irregular meals than those that obtain adequate sleep (56,57,58). Therefore, despite *me time* being important for deactivating the stress response, it may not always be your greatest priority if you are sleep deprived. Determine what your body requires.

Overall, be cautious not to put others' priorities above your own, so that all you have time for is work, caring for others and sleep. Try to have some time for yourself to relax and unwind; to take *me time*.

Find Joy in the Flow

Engaging in *flow activities* can be another way to quieten your mind, enabling you to relax and recharge. Flow activities are activities that engage your full attention so that you become fully absorbed in the activity and time seems to fly. As they say, *time flies when you're having fun*. Incorporating flow activities into your day or week is an effective way to manage stress and to experience joy, and is widely recommended by psychologists.

You may notice some resistance to engaging in flow activities if you are too busy or you have many responsibilities. Engaging in a flow activity doesn't have to take considerable time, just the absorption of your full attention for a period. It's all too easy to waste the little time you do have by scrolling through your Facebook or Instagram feed, vegging out in front of the TV or checking emails.

It is possible that you haven't partaken in a flow activity for such a long time that you've forgotten the feeling. It's a time when all worries and doubts dissolve: where your attention is no longer on your responsibilities and commitments as you master a dance step, a note transition or the pronunciation of a word.

I encourage you to take incremental steps to reignite this feeling, by possibly dedicating fifteen minutes a day (or one hour a week). Consider what you can commit to, reminding yourself that this is time spent to stimulate the relaxation response and shouldn't be another source of stress. The purpose is not to guilt-trip yourself for not partaking in flow activities because you're busy, tired or forgot, but to attempt to do something.

It's possible that you stopped doing an activity you loved because you thought you weren't good enough, or would never make it *professionally*. As a consequence, an activity that once brought much joy may lose its *flow*. For example, say you used to enjoy playing the violin and could escape into the music and feel at one with the instrument. However, when you considered whether you were *good enough* for a performance, or perhaps when you heard someone that was better than you, you started to contemplate

59

the potential of your flow activity turning into a professional pursuit. It is possible that when you turn your flow activity into a competition, performance or product which may be judged by others, the joy disappears. It can cause you to think, *why play the violin, ballroom dance or paint if I'm not going to be the best*; or, *why collect stamps if my collection is worthless*. If you choose to perform, compete or monetise your flow activity, that's perfectly okay. However, be aware of how it influences your state of flow.

You can achieve a state of flow with any activity in which you are fully absorbed. You could find flow in hanging out the washing, washing the dishes or chopping vegetables. It is only your mind that tells you that you should be somewhere else, doing something other than what you're doing right now, which takes you out of the flow. You may believe that you need to *get away* or *escape reality* to reduce stress. However, often it's not reality you want to escape, but the thoughts in your mind. Allow yourself to be swept away by your flow activities or whatever it is you are doing in the moment.

✍ Take up flow activities

What are some activities that you do now or you have done in the past where you were so absorbed that the rest of the world dissolved away? Activities that you enjoy immensely or that simply require considerable focus, so that nothing else enters your mind and you lose track of time?

If you can't think of anything, think back to the things you loved to do as a child or teenager. Did you love to create? Did you love to solve problems or puzzles? Did you enjoy challenging yourself on your own, or partaking in activities that enabled you to connect with others?

Take some time to identify what these activities are for you, and create a list in your Workbook or journal. Included below are some examples of the types of activities you may like to consider. Some of the activities may be chores or painstaking for you and yet bring other people into a state of flow. Everybody has different talents, interests and natural propensities. Each of us is unique.

Creative or artistic pursuits

- art classes, mindfulness colouring or Zentangle
- crafts (e.g. mosaic, sewing, knitting)
- photography
- singing
- drama club
- cooking

Intellectual and developmental pursuits

- learning a language (at home, class, meetups)
- writing or poetry
- book clubs
- jigsaw puzzles
- games or puzzles

cont.

- business or personal development networking groups
- meditation

Physical pursuits

- cycling/running/walking/swimming
- bushwalking group
- gardening
- dancing
- yoga
- Pilates
- juggling
- fitness classes
- exercise videos
- sailing
- surfing/kayaking/canoeing
- rock climbing
- group sports

Take as much time as you require to think of activities to add to your list. Then consider what activities on your list you'd like to commit to this week. Select one activity.

If nothing inspires you right now, or you feel overwhelmed by the thought of engaging in a new activity, continue with the *me time* activities you have engaged in or move on to the next Self-Reflection Activity: *Embrace relaxation techniques*. Alternatively, you may feel less resistance to undertaking a flow activity than embarking on relaxation techniques. Do what feels best to you.

5

Cultivate an Awareness of *What Is*

> *"Your primary purpose is to be here fully, and to be total in whatever you do so that the preciousness of the present moment does not become reduced to a means to an end. And there you have your life purpose. That's the very foundation of your life".*

— Eckhart Tolle

Your thoughts about what you should or shouldn't weigh, what you should or shouldn't eat, and the future consequences of your eating, serve to keep you trapped in diet mentality and the stress response. The thing is, these thoughts are the consequence of resisting the reality of *what is*, the sensory input of sight, sound, smell, taste and touch in the moment.

Resistance to *what is…* promotes stress and anxiety, while accepting *what is…* promotes the relaxation response.

Sensing *What Is*

There are numerous tools employed by psychologists, counsellors and meditation teachers that can help you heighten your awareness of *what is*.

The practice that has supported me most is a regular body scan meditation. I originally used the scan technique developed by Michelle Stanton, of ZoneHigh, called *Sensing what is.* It's specifically designed to relax your body, quieten your mind and heighten your five-sense awareness. Through this or similar mindfulness practices, you can enhance your ability to *listen* to your body and to see things the way they are—*what is*—rather than through the stories your mind constructs.

Although there is no right or wrong way to practise body scan meditations, as with all mindfulness meditation, you'll want to minimise distractions, draw your full awareness to the present moment and observe *what is* without attachment or judgement. Although the intent is to quieten your mind, you have not failed if thoughts arise from time to time. When thoughts arise, witness them like a bird in the sky which passes you by. You notice it, but you don't analyse it or start an internal dialogue of why it is there, and what it means. In this way, you do not create an attachment to the thought.

You may discover that increasing your awareness of *what is* in each moment is not only challenging but alerts you to an internal resistance of bringing your full awareness to the here and now. For instance, you may notice that you put other people's needs above your own as a strategy to resist or avoid what is occurring in the moment. You might do this due to discomfort or because you're feeling unworthy of contentment.

It probably seems that resisting your painful reality would be less uncomfortable than bringing your full awareness to *what is*. However, your avoidance of *what is* preserves the thoughts and beliefs associated with situations or behaviours, rather than enables you to feel and release them fully.

✍ Embrace relaxation techniques

Relaxation techniques, such as mindfulness meditation, body scans or yoga nidra, can help you to relax your body and quieten your mind. It does this through drawing your full awareness to the sensory experience of the moment, rather than being caught up in your thoughts of the past or future. You could choose to do a self-guided meditation (see below) or a guided practice, such as a recording on CD, iTunes, YouTube or Spotify.

Guided relaxation or mindfulness practices can help to start, as they enable you to follow a process—incrementally relaxing and tuning into your body—while minimising distracting thoughts. Practices can be anywhere from five to sixty minutes in duration, so you can choose what fits into your current lifestyle and commitments. It's true that you could commit to a meditation class, however, the purpose of this practice is that it's something you do every day and learn to integrate in your daily life.

If you don't feel you have enough time to commit to five or fifteen minutes a day, consider what might be some barriers to adopting this practice. If time is a true limitation, consider where you could fit a five-minute practice into your day: in your car when you arrive at work or a meeting; in your lunch break; in bed, before you get up; in your car, before you arrive home after work. In these five or fifteen minutes, you could do a self-guided meditation in your mind or listen to a guided body scan with your eyes closed. It's important to have your eyes closed, as it enables you to tune into your other senses without the labelling that occurs when you are distracted by familiar objects.

Take note of any other reasons why you may feel resistance to taking the time for this short practice. Perhaps you can do the Self-Reflection Activity: *Why you may embrace or resist change?* in order to uncover the thoughts and beliefs that might cause you to resist taking up this practice.

cont.

Self-Guided Meditation

Read through the meditation below so that you can repeat the process with your eyes closed, or download it as an audio at www.joyfuleatingnutrition.com/book.

Begin with your body in a comfortable position, either lying on the floor or a bed, or seated on a chair or the floor. Relax your body in your chosen position and close your eyes.

Bring your awareness to your breath. Notice the rise and fall of your chest. Then bring your attention to your breath at your nostrils, noticing the movement of air in and out.

Then relax one body part at a time, from your head to your shoulders, down your arms and fingers, your torso, your legs and into your feet. You may say the name of each body part to yourself while focusing on relaxing it. So, you may say to yourself: eyes relax, nose relax, mouth relax—so that you are repeating the word *relax* for each body part.

Once you have relaxed each body part, bring your awareness to your entire body, and feel your whole body relax. Notice any sensations of *energy* in the body, such as warmth, tingling or pulsating. You may have noticed this with certain body parts, such as the palms of your hands. Imagine this energy surrounding your entire body. You may hold this attention for as long as you like.

When you are ready to discontinue, do so gently and consciously, awakening each sense one at a time. Do so by:

- becoming aware of the space around your body
- noticing the sounds around you, near and far
- noticing any smells
- noticing the taste in your mouth

cont.

- noticing sensations in your body, such as contact with surfaces, air movement or clothing

Gently move your awareness from one sense to the other.

Lastly, gently and slowly open your eyes. Take in the colours, shapes, contrasts and shadows around you, without labelling or judging objects. Look around you with curiosity, as if seeing these objects for the first time. Move your head to take in everything around you. Slowly take everything in, trying to integrate all your senses.

Then begin to move your body—stretch, wriggle—and do whatever movements you require to bring yourself back into full awareness, and to continue with your day.

From time to time throughout the day, try to bring your attention back to the sensory input from your body.

Take a Moment to Stop and Smell the Roses

Not only can you adopt a regular body scan, mindfulness meditation or relaxation practice, you could also take a moment at various times throughout your day to become fully aware of whatever you are doing or what's around you. You could tune into your five senses, and as the saying goes, *stop and smell the roses*. You could take a moment to be fully aware of the feel of sunshine or breeze on your skin, the sensations of washing the dishes or your hair, grass under your feet, or eating a juicy piece of ripe fruit.

When your mind becomes consumed by a thought or you become tense as a result of thinking, try to bring your awareness back to your body. Draw your attention to bodily sensations, such as: your breath at your stomach, chest or nostrils; your feet in contact with the floor; your buttocks on a chair; the sensation of clothing or air movement against your skin; the sounds around you; tastes in your mouth; or aromas in the air surrounding you.

6

Accept *What Is*

> *"Accept—then act. Whatever the present moment contains, accept it as if you had chosen it. Always work with it, not against it."*

> — Eckhart Tolle

It's widely believed that you need to resist your body as it is (*what is*) to get motivated to commence and stick to a desired change or action. Sure, it's true that discontentment with your current circumstances and thus a resistance to *what is* can result in taking action. But I believe that action taken in this way can result in you fighting against reality, attempting to control your eating, weight, body, situations and people in your life. And this, unfortunately, may stimulate the stress response and thus sabotage your health and happiness.

So, how do you accept *what is*? Accepting *what is* requires acceptance of the reality of this moment as witnessed through the five senses: sight, sound, smell, taste and touch. It's acceptance of the reality of the situation without labelling, analysing, explaining or judging it. It's acceptance of *what is* in the present moment, rather than thoughts of the past, or future implications. It's acknowledging that fighting against the reality of *what is* in this moment—and guilt-tripping yourself—is not going to change it. As the saying goes, *don't cry over spilt milk*. What is done is done, and no amount of thinking otherwise can change *what is*: *it is as it is*.

Acceptance of *what is* does not imply that your life will be *all roses*, but that no matter what unfolds you can witness it with your full awareness, non-attachment and non-judgement. Nor does acceptance of *what is* imply inaction, but merely acceptance that you cannot change *what is* through your thinking.

Accepting Your Body as It Is

You may feel that you can accept the sensory input in this moment, however, accepting your body as it is right now might seem like something else entirely. You may feel resistance to accepting *what is* because you've been led to believe that discontentment and dissatisfaction with your current body weight or size will motivate you to change. However, I've found that resisting your body as it is right now is what can lead you to: set unrealistic expectations; declare that you won't consume any more chocolate or have alcohol until the diet is over; yo-yo diet, compulsively eat, secretly eat, or sabotage your efforts in any multitude of ways.

The notion of accepting your body as it is may seem inconceivable if you are clinically considered overweight, have been diagnosed with a health condition, or you simply detest your body. The thing is, your thoughts, discontentment and resistance to *what is*, in no way change *what is* in this moment.

The weight or size you are right now is exactly as it is meant to be in this moment. Right now, you weigh what you weigh, and no amount of thinking otherwise, resisting it, self-reprimanding, punishing yourself, guilt or shame is going to change your weight or health right now.

Let's say you receive a diagnosis of diabetes. Should you have diabetes in this moment? Yes, because you have diabetes. No amount of cursing and reprimanding about what you did in the past or what the future consequences may be, will stop you from having diabetes right now. *It is as it is.*

When you resist your body as it is right now, you are perpetuating distrust in your body. You are reinforcing the belief that it should be other than it is in this moment. However, your thoughts do not control your weight and health in this moment. Your weight and health are the consequence of your biology, genetics, past actions and behaviours, socioeconomic environment and level of stress.

Considering this, you may feel guilt and blame for having *let yourself go* in the past; for *allowing* yourself to get to where you are right now. However, what has happened has happened, and resisting it in this moment does not change it right now. Resistance to *what is* does more to perpetuate stress, anxiety, guilt and shame, than serve you to care for yourself.

Let's explore some common fears and misconceptions associated with accepting your body as it is.

Accepting what is does not imply inaction

Accepting *what is* does not imply that you are giving up and settling for *what is,* or that you'll take no action to improve your health or life circumstances. It certainly doesn't imply that your body will stay the way it is right now forever, where you may think, *why bother I'll never change.* When you accept *what is*—rather than fighting and forcing yourself, wishing your situation to be other than it is, feeling defeated or that you are a victim of *what is*—you accept that you cannot change anything in this moment through your thinking.

Feeling sorry for yourself, thinking that this shouldn't have happened, that it's so unfair, or feeling guilty for your part in your current situation… does not serve you in moving forward. Despite the frequent use of self-shame and self-deprecating thoughts as a motivator, these are hindrances. They hold you in a pattern of thinking: *I'm not good enough, I'm a failure, I'm not worthy of success, love and happiness.* When you accept your current situation, you can create space for limitless potentialities in the next moment.

So, rather than occupying your mind with thoughts about past mistakes or future consequences, focus on what you can do now. You can accept the reality of *what is* in this moment and then ask yourself, *now what? Now, how will I respond or act in this situation, towards this person or with this condition?* You can think: *I am so and so kilograms: it is as it is, now what? I have diabetes: it is as it is, now what? I can't fit into the dresses in my wardrobe: it is as it is, now what?*

This doesn't mean you are giving up. But, instead, you're liberating yourself from the thoughts that cause you stress and emotional distress. Then, in the following moment, you can take inspired action, without the stress and struggle that originates from resisting *what is*. Therefore, accepting *what is* involves letting go of attaching your happiness and contentment to achieving your goals. This enables you to feel content with what you have right now, which is not necessarily the result of loving *what is* but rather no longer resisting, fighting and trying to control it.

Accepting your body without the labels and stories

Accepting *what is*, is not about accepting the labels you or society have imposed on you, such as *I am fat* or *I am unhealthy*. Nor is it accepting the stories you may associate with these labels, such as *I am fat, and I will be for the rest of my life. I've got no self-control, so I may as well accept myself as I am. I'm a diabetic, there's nothing I can do about it. I clearly can't stick to a diet, so why bother?* These are stories, conclusions, assumptions, implications and consequences that your mind has associated and attached to *what is*. They are not your reality. Accepting *what is*, is accepting the reality of all five-senses rather than your thoughts and interpretations of *what is*.

Accepting your body doesn't mean you'll 'let it go'

You may fear you'll *let yourself go* if you accept your body as it is. Experience may have led you to believe that you cannot trust yourself around food without a diet or eating plan. However, your perceived lack of control around food, experienced as overeating, compulsive eating or binge eating, is likely the result of immense hunger, restriction and deprivation due to dieting; not a failing of your body or a lack of willpower.

71

You don't require control over your body to prevent weight gain or to maintain good health. You can take action focused on how the change feels—physically, mentally and emotionally—without attachment to achieving an end goal.

Accepting your body doesn't mean you have to love it

Inspirational quotes encouraging you to *love your body* are appearing on social media and other online platforms, including advertising messages for clothing, sporting goods and beauty products. Although these messages have an explicitly positive intent, they're often accompanied by images of people with flawless skin, tanned and sculpted bodies, in unattainable yoga poses.

These messages often miss the mark for the average person or people in larger bodies. The read-between-the-lines message is that if you love your body, your body will love you back by endowing you with a gorgeous body. These messages and images, unfortunately, reinforce the belief that a healthy body is a beautiful body and do little to shift the perception of what health truly is.

In parallel, there has been an increase in bloggers, speakers and comedians that are considered *fat activists*, who aspire to share messages about accepting all bodies. These messages and efforts are helpful in reducing *fat shaming* and opening people's minds to the spectrum of body types. They also play an important role in shifting the narrow perspective of what is beautiful and healthy. While I sincerely hope that size diversity becomes more accepted by the wider public and health professionals, I recognise that if you've been struggling with your weight for years, you may feel there is a huge impassable canyon between hating your body and loving it.

Unfortunately, positive messages of size diversity and fat acceptance may do little to quieten the voice in your head that has been shaming you for many years. Undeniably, external messages and the wider perception of weight, body shape and size can play a considerable role in your perception of yourself. However, acceptance starts with you. Acceptance begins with you accepting yourself and your body as it is.

Acceptance of your body doesn't mean that you necessarily love your body, but that you no longer fight against it. Loving your body needn't become another goal you strive for.

If at this point, you still desire weight loss don't be ashamed of this either. Accept your desire for weight loss if it remains. You'll hold onto this desire until it no longer serves you. However, recognise that it's more socially acceptable to put yourself down than to be perceived as narcissistic. Accepting yourself can, therefore, seem self-indulgent. Nevertheless, when you recognise that you can only experience the world and express yourself through the one body that you have, it is not self-indulgent or selfish to care for yourself, it is imperative.

Accepting your current health status

You may be unsure how you can accept your body as it is if you are unwell or have a serious or undesirable health condition. Accepting *what is*, is accepting that you have specific symptoms, which no regret, guilt, shame or blame can change in this moment.

Accepting *what is*, is also not identifying with an illness, such as *I am a diabetic*. Instead, you are accepting that you have a health condition in this moment and that it does not define who you are as a person. If you self-identify with your health condition, it can perpetuate feelings of defeatism.

As well, resolving your symptoms or health status may threaten who you are. You may fear who you will become and how people will interact with you when you no longer have these issues. Therefore, although you may want to resolve your health concerns, you may feel a resistance to change, as being a part of this select group provides some benefit or solidarity. Consequently, you may find yourself sabotaging your efforts.

It can be incredibly difficult to accept *what is* when you lose your sense of identity. That said, it is only a perception of who you are, created by attaching your identity to the things that you can and cannot do. Thus, if you're *robbed* of your health or full use of your physical or mental faculties, you not only grieve this loss but are left with the uncertainty of who you are, without the labels you or society had previously placed on you.

Let me explain by sharing my father's story of accepting his health status. My father was diagnosed with cardiomyopathy before he reached sixty. The doctors were baffled as to how someone of his age, in otherwise good health, could have this condition, as cardiomyopathy is a degenerative heart disease more common in older adults.

My father had been an active person his entire life. He has built houses, carried bags of cement over his shoulder and chopped firewood. Now he has slowed to a snail's pace, where walking up a flight of stairs is a struggle. He's had to accept not being able to ride his bicycle, backpack through Vietnam, or be *Mr Fix-it* around the house. He often has to explain himself to others, as although he looks healthy, there are things he can't do. When he became a grandfather, he had to explain that there were certain things he couldn't or wasn't prepared to do. He couldn't carry a birthday cake from the fridge to the backyard, lift a stroller out of the car, or move a box of blocks from a child's bedroom to the living room.

At his checkups in the first few years after his diagnosis, his doctors would ask him how he was feeling. They asked how he felt, because it was not uncommon for people with his condition to feel depressed. Dad would say, 'I just need to accept what I can't do and learn what I can do'. Although he would love to feel the exhilaration of air rushing against his face as he coasts down a hill on his bicycle after the strenuous effort to the top, he knows that he can't. He has chosen not to resist the reality of his situation but to accept it.

Having a debilitating health condition or being in severe pain can make it more challenging to be present in the moment and accept *what is*. The thing is, it is your mind that *says* you should be somewhere else, doing something else: *I should not be feeling pain; I have so much work to do I can't afford to be bedridden; I should have taken better care of myself.*

Unfortunately, no amount of thinking will change your situation in this moment. Your resistance to *what is* may inadvertently intensify your physical symptoms as a consequence of drawing your attention to what you don't want. It may also activate the stress response, possibly influencing nutrient uptake, blood sugar, blood pressure and inflammation in your body.

Accepting *what is* doesn't mean that you ignore pain or other physical sensations, but that you don't attach thoughts and emotions that serve no purpose other than to cause you emotional distress. When you are emotionally distressed, it can reduce your ability to think rationally and constructively. It can cause you to take action or make decisions in a panicked and confused state of mind. Conversely, when you accept that you are feeling pain in this moment, you can calmly take the next action steps to improve your physical state, without the must-achieve mentality that perpetuates stress and anxiety.

✍ Actively accept your body as it is right now

To embrace *what is*, let's remove the visual cues in your home that remind you that your body is not the way you want it to be. You may think that holding onto those *skinny* jeans that you fit into twenty years ago, or before your last diet, are a motivator. At times they may appear to be. Yet, at other times they may cause you to feel inadequate or a failure. These clothes may lead you to believe that you are kidding yourself in wishing for something that's seemingly out of reach. Even if you get close to achieving your goals, they are a reminder that you still aren't *there*. Rather than motivate you, they may deflate your mood every time you go to choose an outfit for the day. Therefore, I encourage you to search your home for visual cues that remind you that you're not the weight or size you want to be.

In the kitchen

What's lurking in your kitchen cupboards that you don't currently use, which remind you that you are not the weight or size you want to be? Perhaps there are:

- *meal replacements* that you didn't enjoy and were not satisfying
- *diet pills* that you never opened or ones that didn't fulfil their promises
- *kitchen scales* you bought when on a previous diet program
- *calorie counting or diet books* that you've never used or don't contain tempting recipes
- *'healthy' foods that you don't enjoy* but purchased because they are low-fat or low-calorie

Remove these items from your kitchen, preferably throwing them out or giving them away. Let go of holding onto these items *just in case*. They only serve to keep you trapped in diet mentality.

cont.

In the bathroom

Take your *scales* and throw them out! Alternatively, give them away or take a hammer to them: whatever you feel will signify putting an end to them dictating your mood. If you're not ready to dispose of your scales, tuck them away in a hard-to-reach place, such as a cupboard or out of sight in the garage. Your scales, again, are a reminder that you aren't the weight you want to be.

Check the bathroom cupboards for any diet pills, weight loss body wraps or cellulite reducing devices and potions. Dispose of anything that's a diet or figure-forming product, or any other products you haven't use in the past 12 months. You may also like to rearrange products in your bathroom so that those that represent self-nurturing are in easy reach or displayed as reminders, such as bubble bath, essential oils, massage oil, moisturiser or candles.

In the wardrobe

Now open your wardrobe and take a look at your clothes, without judgement of your current weight or size. Sort through your clothes and place them into two piles: those that currently fit you and those that used to.

Of the clothes that currently fit you, if there is anything that makes you feel especially *fat and frumpy*—put it straight into a donate pile. Only keep well-fitting clothes that:

• are of colours, patterns and styles that you feel good in

• make you feel confident, comfortable, and

• you often receive compliments when you wear them.

cont.

Keep some comfy clothes for around the house but follow the above criteria for clothing you plan to wear outside of your home. If you're not particularly happy with the clothes that currently fit you, explore ways you can dress them up, say using scarves, jewellery or belts. If there isn't anything in your current size you love, go shopping. If going clothes shopping is a daunting prospect, remember that your aim is to feel good as you are right now.

Now to the pile of clothes that you used to fit into. You definitely don't want to see these clothes every day. So, either ditch them, donate them or hide them way out of sight. When assessing this pile, consider:

1. <u>Those that are too large</u>: are reminders of a time you were a larger size than you are now. It may be that you don't want to be this size again, or you have lost considerable weight (due to illness or excessive dieting) and would like to gain this weight back, as you felt more healthy and vibrant at this larger size. If the latter is true, and you may potentially gain the weight back, put these clothes together in a bag or suitcase out of everyday view. If you didn't feel vibrant and well when you fitted into these larger clothes, you might want to dump them or donate them.

2. <u>Those that are too small</u>: but felt particularly stunning on you, along with super comfortable and confident. Preferably let them go as they continue to serve as reminders of a desire to lose weight. If you can't face letting them go, then keep them in a box or suitcase out of sight, such as the back of your wardrobe or a cupboard you don't frequent often. If they don't fit you in 12 months time, ditch or donate them.

3. <u>Those that are too small</u>: that were never that flattering or comfortable and are nothing special. Dump or donate them.

cont.

> **Journal the process**
>
> During the above process, negative thoughts and emotions may arise about your body. Or you may become aware of past or current preconceptions of dieting and weight management. Take note of these in your journal.
>
> If you feel overwhelmed by the process, discontinue it and come back to it later. However, take some time to reflect on why you feel overwhelmed, and why you may be resisting the process.
>
> Record in your Workbook or journal the emotions and thoughts that arose through this activity, whether they be *negative* or you feel a sense of liberation and acceptance for your body as it is.

Accepting *What Is* isn't Positive Thinking

Many self-help proponents talk about the value of practising positive thinking and affirmations. They suggest that through these practices you'll attract more positive experiences into your life. Although undeniably more beneficial than thinking negatively about your life circumstances or others behaviours, it differs from accepting *what is*.

The practices of positive thinking and affirmations can create an expectation that things will turn out for the best, and thus are essentially goal setting in disguise. This is because the underlying hope is that these practices will generate positive outcomes. How often when something goes wrong in life do you or others put a positive spin on it: *every cloud has a silver lining; good things come to those who wait; nothing worth having comes easy; everything will work out for the best; there are no shortcuts to any place worth going; all the hard work will be worth it.* This positive spin implies that your *pain* will be for something. That if things are tough right now, it will get better and you'll be rewarded for your efforts. However, you cannot know this to be true.

In contrast, accepting *what is*, is accepting what has occurred in your life without spinning it into a positive or a negative. It's not about seeing the glass as half full or half empty, but seeing it as it is: neither positive nor negative.

It's possible that trying to put a positive spin on things can cause you to suppress your emotions or downplay the depth of your emotional distress. When you experience emotions that you don't believe you should, like anger or disappointment, not only may you potentially suppress them, it may well generate additional feelings of guilt and shame for feeling these negative emotions, since you are supposed to be positive.

Furthermore, the practice of affirmations can feel incongruent to how you feel. You may wake in the morning and say to yourself in the mirror, *I am powerful, confident and capable*, when in fact you feel like crawling back into bed or just plodding through the day without drawing attention to yourself. To have days like this is completely normal. The thing is, when you perceive that you *should* be able to always maintain a positive mindset, it can be disheartening when you don't, or when you feel the affirmation you recite to yourself is a blatant lie. If you feel sluggish, unenthused or bored, rather than spurring you on, practising positive thinking and affirmations can cause you to feel like a fraud: that you are fooling yourself and everyone else in your life that you are powerful, confident and capable.

Accepting the Unknown

It's possible that what you perceive as *good* in one moment may no longer be considered *good* in the next. You may perceive a situation or behaviour as *wrong* or *bad*, but then as further events transpire, you realise that it was good when considering the entire situation or your whole life. Hence, with hindsight, your perception of whether an event is good or bad changes.

The reason that your perception can change with hindsight is that you witness your life moment to moment. When you experience each moment, you cannot see what will unfold in the next. In this way, it's as if you live your life through a telescopic lens, where your view is limited to the detail of the current moment.

In the current moment, the situation can feel all-consuming, overwhelming, tragic, frightening, painful, and as if it will never end. However, life experience has shown you that, *this too shall pass*, as everything does.

If you could zoom out from this moment to your entire life—extending from birth to death—the current situation or event may merely be a notch in your lifespan. So that, a single situation or event that you perceive as bad when viewed over the context of your entire life, may be perceived as good. It's not that the situation or event is either good or bad, but that your attempt to categorise it as such is futile, as your perception will most probably change over the course of your life.

Hence, despite a perception that your current weight is undesirable or unhealthy, you cannot absolutely know whether your weight is good or bad in this moment—*it* simply *is as it is*. When you zoom out across your entire lifespan, you may discover the role your weight and body issues have played in the unfolding of your life. You may even discover that your struggles with food and your body weight and size enabled you to grow and learn, and presented opportunities that would never have arisen without them. This is not to imply that your struggles with food and your body are good or positive, but that it is unknown.

You don't need to be able to predict the future to accept *what is,* right now. Believing that you can influence the future through your thoughts only serves to perpetuate worry and anxiety. Consideration of every possible outcome in your mind doesn't really prepare you for the worst-case scenario but instead can cause you to live many reiterations of possible worst-case scenarios in your mind, over and over.

And unfortunately, your body doesn't distinguish between reality and your thoughts, and thus your thoughts create the same physiological and psychological changes in your body as if the event *has* occurred. Instead of being prepared for what unfolds, you are likely exhausted and anxious, and potentially less alert and present should the worst-case scenario arise.

When you accept *what is,* you can respond to whatever situations arise with a clarity of mind and calmness. You can then ask yourself, *now what?*

Now, what steps will you take in this moment, if you so desire, which may or may not change the direction of your life? You are not privy to either hindsight or foresight, so you can only take the action that feels appropriate and favourable in each moment.

Accepting all Aspects of Yourself

Accepting *what is* encompasses acceptance of all of yourself, rather than just those aspects that you like or are comfortable with. Accepting *what is* involves that you:

- **Accept your current weight** or size without resistance, shame, blame, self-reprimanding or resigning yourself to it being this way forever. Accept your body in this moment, without attachment to the labels or preconceived notions of what your weight or size should or should not be. In this moment your weight is what your weight is; *it is as it is.*

- **Accept your current health** without guilt or blame, without labels that are only your perception of *what is,* and are not the absolute truth. Accept your health without resigning yourself to the belief that you cannot change your health. Accept it as if you chose it and then ask yourself, *now what?*

- **Accept your circumstances** without thinking they should be another way, or that they dictate your future. *It is as it is, now what?*

- **Accept your past** without thinking that this should or should not have happened, that you will never change, or that your fate is sealed no matter what you do. Instead, acknowledge that what has occurred has occurred. *It is as it is, now what?*

- **Accept other people's behaviours**, comments and thoughts because they have nothing to do with you, but simply reflect their beliefs and perspective of the world. This doesn't imply that you allow others to treat you disrespectfully or put you in danger, but that you cannot control anyone else's behaviours, comments and thoughts. Attempting to do so can intensify the situation. Your ability to accept other people starts with acceptance of yourself, just as you are.

- **Accept your emotions** without the thought that you should not be feeling the way you are feeling. The way you feel is the way you feel; *it is as it is.* When you for example think, *I shouldn't feel this way, it's been five years,* or *others have had it tougher, I should get over myself,* you're resisting *what is,* instead of accepting how you feel in this moment. Likewise, putting a positive spin on a situation can do more to conceal or ignore your emotions in the moment.

- **Accept compliments** without shaking them off, twisting their meaning or making them conditional on the situation or person providing the compliment. Accepting *what is* means accepting the appreciation someone shows you, without attachment to the thoughts that you are good or bad. Nor is it engaging in internal dialogue, such as, *she only said I did a good job to make me feel better for being the fattest on the team,* or *she said I look good in this dress because I normally don't look great,* or *he'd be more complementary if the dress were a few sizes smaller.* It's only your thoughts that cause you to believe that you don't deserve a compliment or induce guilt for receiving praise. Someone else's perspective is based on their own beliefs and has nothing to do with you.

Accepting *what is,* is acknowledging that no amount of thinking, fighting or resisting *what is* will change *what is* in this moment. There may be certain situations, events or people's behaviour that you find hard to accept. Yet acceptance isn't about no responsibility; there are laws and etiquette we must all abide by.

Acceptance in every instance, whether considering law-abiding action or not, firstly involves your awareness of the sensory input of the moment. It is then the thoughts and stories your mind makes up that can take you out of the moment and potentially cause you to respond in a non-constructive way. If you're resisting *what is,* your response may be fuelled with irritation, anger, panic or volatility, rather than being calm and focused. It may be that the most empowering thing you can do in any moment is accept *what is,* and then ask yourself, *now what?*

7

Release the Illusion of Control

"The primary cause of unhappiness is never the situation but thought about it. Be aware of the thoughts you are thinking. Separate them from the situation, which is always neutral.

It is as it is."

— Eckhart Tolle

Dieting is founded on the belief that you can control your body through your actions. However, it is this perception of control that may sabotage your weight loss and health goals. Let me illustrate with a client's experience.

This lady's weight had slowly increased in the five years following a divorce. She was concerned that the weight gain might be due to hormonal changes, as she'd turn 40 in this period. However, none of the tests that her doctor undertook revealed any medical issues.

I was curious as to why the weight crept on following the divorce. I asked her what changes in her thinking had occurred as a consequence. It seems that once she was living on her own, she thought: *I am a strong independent woman, and I don't need a man to make me happy. I now have the freedom to live exactly how I want, on my own terms. I can now control what I eat and when I eat.*

This perception of control was initially empowering and initiated her into the world of dieting and personal training. However, in tandem, her weight slowly increased. It may have been a coincidence, but it appeared that her weight gain was connected with her attempt to control her body and eating.

I asked her if she would be open to relaxing her eating rules and stop pushing herself so hard with her intense exercise program. So she embraced eating consciously. She relaxed about eating out with friends and going out for work lunches. We spent time in our sessions exploring her perception and fear of being dependant on a man. Although our focus wasn't weight loss, she re-established her pre-divorce weight within one year.

I don't share this lady's story to pronounce promises of weight loss. In fact, I've had clients who have followed a similar process and, despite achieving contentment with their body and eating, did not lose weight. The purpose of sharing this client's experience is to emphasise that your attempts to control your eating and body may well be what's sabotaging your weight and health. Contrary to what you've been led to believe: that you need to establish control over your eating, exercise and lifestyle behaviours to maintain a healthy weight, the opposite may be true.

> your attempts to control your eating and body may well be what's sabotaging your weight and health.

The belief that you can control your body through what you eat and the exercise you do is reinforced by diet and health proponents that share their *after* body images online. Some go on to assert that they resolved copious ailments through their regime of eating or exercising. They create an illusion that they carved out their current *gorgeous bikini body*, and that you too can do the same with hard work and dedication. Yet, how their body responded to the actions they took is unique to them. It is their genetic predisposition that enabled them to achieve a *gorgeous bikini body* with their regime of green smoothies and intense yoga poses. However, green smoothies and yoga classes, although healthful behaviours, are unlikely to give you their body, as you too are unique. They don't control the body they have, just as you do not, either.

You Do Not Control Your Body

It is an illusion that you control your body. Firstly, you don't control your genetics. It's not like you got to *select* your body, such as the colour of your skin or width of your hip bones. You didn't control the family or socioeconomic environment you were born into, whether you were breastfed, or the foods you were introduced to as an infant. Nor do you control the rules around eating and movement you were exposed to by your parents, teachers or peers.

Secondly, though you choose what you eat and how you move your body, you don't control how your body responds to this input. Your body deconstructs everything you eat. It absorbs, transports, integrates and stores the nutrition you provide it, without your conscious effort. Everything you eat becomes *you* on a cellular level and enables you to live your life. However, you have no control over these processes or any other processes in your body. You don't control your heartbeat, your breath or the release of hormones that regulate hunger, satiety, metabolism, and numerous other functions in your body. You don't control the nerve impulses to every cell, your body's ability to fight off disease, and cell replication occurring within your body right now.

When you accept that you have no control over your body, despite your best intentions and actions, you can relax and respond to life as it unfolds, without attempting to control *what is*. You can adopt behaviours to improve your well-being, without believing that you are a failure if the outcomes you expected do not eventuate. If your health declines, you can accept it without blame and regret. Instead, you can embrace actions that feel good to your body and reduce associated symptoms, without pressure and stress.

Years ago, when I'd step on the scales or suck in my stomach in front of the mirror, I'd think to myself: *I'm doing great, this diet (or exercise regime) appears to be working. If I keep this up, imagine how I'll look.* This thinking would cause me to restrict my diet further, or exercise harder. It was as if the more I felt in control, the more control I wanted. However, this would lead my eating to *spiral out of control*, as I'd become so hungry that I'd end up overeating. Or I ended up unable to exercise, due to fatigue or muscle soreness from overtraining. This thinking is not unlike what people with eating disorders experience except to an amplified intensity.

You're likely to have your own perception and relationship to control. You may feel that your eating or body is completely out of control, and thus you desire some semblance of control. Alternatively, you may feel in control when you are dieting, but fear that once you quit and allow yourself to eat without restriction, your weight will *balloon* out of control. Even if you can maintain control, it may be at the expense of enjoying life, as you are constantly thinking and feeling anxious about food.

Whether you feel like you have your eating or body under control, or feel completely out of control, it is the perception of control that keeps you locked in diet mentality. Yet, you do not control your body.

You Do Not Control Your Eating

You may be able to appreciate that you don't control how your body responds to food, but continue to believe that you control what you eat. However, your relationship with food is complicated. You don't control the foods you were exposed to as an infant and child, foods which influence your taste preferences and food associations. You don't control whether you like chocolate or vanilla ice cream. Nor whether toasted cheese sandwiches, macaroni cheese, chicken soup or roast potatoes are comforting foods for you. You don't control the opinions of your family or society; these shape your beliefs about food, such as what you perceive as pleasurable, indulgent, rewarding, healthy or unhealthy, and so on. Therefore, despite the impression that *you* choose (and thus control) what to or not to eat, your choices and behaviours are influenced by the totality of your food experiences.

You Do Not Control Your Thoughts

The belief that you control your thoughts is an illusion: thoughts arise in your mind without your control. Try it. Try to control every thought that arises in your mind for the next hour. It's impossible. Thoughts enter your mind without your control.

Once you think a thought, you can choose to ignore it or act on it. It is this choice that can be perceived as an ability to control *what is*.

Nonetheless, how you interpret the thoughts that arise in your mind are a consequence of your past experiences and conditioning, which are all completely out of your control. You never chose your natural talents, your parents, the culture you were born into, the school you attended, your interests, and so on. Therefore, despite it appearing that you choose how you interpret and act on a thought—as you employ logic and rationality to make decisions—the way you interpret and perceive the world is out of your control.

I'm not saying that you are not accountable. You are still accountable to the law and must follow appropriate etiquette at work and in society. However, being accountable doesn't require control. It requires knowledge, experience and an awareness of *what is*.

You may be able to reflect on a time when you acted to avert danger or provide protection, without having to stop and consider the best approach to take in the moment. This action may have almost appeared immediate or impulsive. Thoughts were obviously present, but they would've occurred in quick succession and without consideration of every possible scenario and approach. In such emergency situations, the brain is capable of rapidly drawing on experiences, knowledge and procedures to enable you to act appropriately and without delay.

Conversely, unrelenting thought can cause deliberation, worry, uncertainty and second-guessing of the best approach. It can impede action or cause you to act in a state of panic or anxiety. In this state, your decision making and efficiency may be diminished.

Moreover, the belief that you have control influences how you feel moment-to-moment. When you perceive that you are in control, you can feel capable, successful, righteous, triumphant, proud or victorious. Conversely, when you perceive that you've lost control, you can feel ashamed, disappointed, frustrated, resentful and defeated. As such, your perception of control can influence both your mood and activation of the stress response.

Liberating yourself of control can enable you to embrace your life in a more spontaneous and inspired way. It can allow you to be present in each moment, without the internal dialogue that serves only to cause you emotional distress. It can take time and reflection on numerous experiences to deeply appreciate that you don't control your body, your eating or your thoughts, since this sense of control is what you've been led to believe your entire life.

✍ Learning that you've no control

To help you grasp that you do not control your eating, your body or your thoughts, for one week, note down each day something over which you had no control. It could be an unexpected phone call, someone you had an uplifting conversation with at the supermarket or an unexpected birthday cake brought into work. For example:

- I don't control that I didn't hear the alarm
- I don't control that my husband ate all of my favourite cereal
- I don't control that I got a call from my sister about our catch up on the weekend
- I don't control that I received an email confirming my massage appointment this evening
- I don't control the busy traffic on the way home from work

If you feel emotional distress concerning the events you note, try to identify the thoughts that follow and record them in your Workbook or journal. So, for the above examples, you may have thought to yourself:

- *I should have set the alarm louder or earlier. I am so forgetful.*
- *I should have purchased more cereal. My husband knows that it's my favourite, I can't believe he ate it all. Doesn't he respect me?*
- *My sister shouldn't have called me before my workday started. I shouldn't have answered the phone.*
- *I'm so pleased I booked that massage, how clever am I? I so deserve spoiling myself. That was so self-indulgent to book a massage. I don't have the time. There are so many other things I need to do this evening.*
- *I should have taken another route home. Now I'm going to be late for the massage. What if I lose my down-payment? That's money wasted. I don't have money to throw around. I should be less frivolous with my spending. If I don't manage my money better, I'll never be able to retire.*

Thoughts that you control *what is* do more to cause you emotional distress, than change what has happened. When you accept *what is* and release your perception or desire for control, you can take action in a clear and calm way; *it is as it is, now what?*

8

Accepting Who You Are, as You Are

*"When you judge a woman by her appearance,
it doesn't define her, it defines you."*

— Steve Maraboli, *Unapologetically You: Reflections
on Life and the Human Experience*

I recall an occasion when I went to the park to eat my lunch by the ocean on a weekday. I walked past a lady sitting at a picnic table facing out to sea. She looked up and saw me—a complete stranger. I smiled at her. Rather than say hello, she smiled at me and said, 'I don't normally eat like this for lunch'. I looked at the table and only then noticed that she was eating fish and chips. She clearly felt a need to explain her eating to me, possibly because she was ashamed or embarrassed by her food choice, and feared that I would judge her.

You too may have felt the need to explain or justify your eating to others, whether dining companions, waiting staff or strangers, for fear of judgement.

Liberate Yourself from the Fear of Judgement

Fear of judgement stems from a perception that *how you look* defines *who you are*. It can affect your confidence so much that you might hide behind a façade of who you think you need to be, to be accepted by others. Despite your best attempts, you cannot control others' perception of you, and each person will perceive you differently. Thus, it will always be a losing battle. The way to liberate yourself from fear of judgement is to start with how you judge yourself and others. This is because judgement breeds judgement. Let me explain with an example.

Say you see a woman in a swimsuit and think to yourself, *she really shouldn't be wearing that; it's unflattering. If I were that large, I wouldn't go swimming.* Then, you see an incredibly *skinny woman*, whose hip bones are protruding through her one-piece, and think to yourself; *she's way too thin, that's not attractive at all.* Although this comparison may be in an attempt to either feel better about your body or to determine what to aspire to, it does more to contribute to your fear that others will judge you. This is because when you step out in your swimsuit, you are likely to fear being judged. Or you may not swim at all, although you'd love to.

Sadly, being a h*ealthy weight* or a desirable body shape or size does not shield you from others judgement or your own fear of being judged. Say a woman of what others may perceive as a desirable weight walks into a weight loss group, and you think to yourself, *what's she doing here, she's not overweight.* The thing is, just by looking at her you can't know her story, her relationship with food and body, or how she perceives herself. You don't know what's going through her mind. You don't know what she sees when she looks in the mirror. You don't know if she's always been this weight or size. You don't know if she binges or deprives herself, or obsesses about food every waking moment. You don't know whether you may have more in common with her than not. Quite simply, you cannot accurately judge any person based on their appearance.

If you do judge others by their size, dress sense, haircut, driving skills, phone manner, and so on, you are doing more to fuel your own concern that others will judge you. It's only when you stop judging yourself and others, that you will become less preoccupied with others judgment of you. This doesn't mean that others will no longer judge you... because they will continue to do so. However, you can recognise that how others perceive you is completely subjective and out of your control—as the saying goes, *beauty is in the eye of the beholder.*

When you release your fear of being judged for your weight, it can appear that those around you judge you less for it. This is because if you believe others' perception of you is based on your weight, you may interpret a second glance your way, a query into your diet, or a comment about how good something looks on you, as solely attributable to your weight and shape. However, you don't know why someone gave you a second glance; they might actually like your blouse.

> When you release your fear of being judged for your weight, it can appear that those around you judge you less for it.

In other instances, you may know outright that a person's perception of you is based on your weight. For example, you may have received snide remarks or comments concerning your weight, size or eating; received unsolicited advice about diet, exercise or appropriate attire; or been rejected by a sports coach or romantic interest due to your weight. Other people's comments on your weight and eating can hurt. Yet it's only that person's perception of who you are. Their thoughts are founded on their belief system and have nothing to do with you.

The reason that what others say often hurts is because your deepest fears are being mirrored back to you in their remarks or glances. Yet, as you begin to accept your body as it is and recognise that others' glances or comments about you have nothing to do with you, and are completely out of your control, their remarks and glances will phase you less. When they do cause you emotional angst, or you feel others' comments or behaviours are inappropriate or inconsiderate, instead of responding in an emotionally charged way, you can rebut them in a calmer and more considered manner.

Disassociating from judgemental people or influences, such as magazines and social media, can be helpful to reduce your tendency to judge yourself or others. However, no matter your weight or size, judgement will persist. You can't escape it.

Attempting to evade others' judgement can cause you to consume much of your time trying to be who you think others want you to be. It can cause you to become a *people pleaser*. It can lead you to avoid conflict or bury your anger. Consequently, you can lose your true identity in the person you are trying to be so as to meet other people's expectations. Remember, you are more than your body, weight or size, and it is only one facet of who you are, although admittedly one on which others may judge you. What others think of you has more bearing on who *they are* than who you are.

There are many aspects to your personality—and your weight or dress size is not one of them.

✍ Explore your judgement of eating and body

Let's explore how you judge yourself and others, and how you perceive that others judge you, based on weight, size and eating.

Activity 1. Judgement of weight or size

In this activity, consider two categories:

- what you perceive as a desirable weight or size
- what you perceive as an undesirable weight or size

One of the categories may relate to your own weight or size right now. For the other, you'll have to imagine what it might be like to be this weight or size, and how you would perceive that. For these two categories, consider your judgement of your own and other people's weight or size, plus how you think others would judge you based on your weight or size.

It can be useful to see your thoughts in a table format so that you can compare the categories side by side. An example table is provided below; you could either complete the judgement table in your companion Workbook or copy it into your journal. Record all the thoughts that come to mind, no matter how trivial they may seem. In the tables, I've included some example thoughts that may prompt you and give you an idea of what to record.

cont.

	Judgement of **self**	My judgement of **others**	How I think others judge **me**
Desirable weight or Size	e.g. I have good discipline. e.g. I'm so good for maintaining this diet.	e.g. She must be so happy and confident being her perfect weight. e.g. She's so self-centred wearing that sports bra to the gym.	e.g. She's so lucky to be able to maintain a healthy weight. e.g. She's weak, as she needs to maintain her beauty to keep a man or her self-worth.
Undesirable Weight or Size	e.g. My body has betrayed me. e.g. I've got no self-discipline, others can stick to an exercise regime, why can't I?	e.g. She's got a pretty face, that's why she's not ashamed to be a fat advocate. e.g. She shouldn't show so much flesh.	e.g. She is so lazy. e.g. She must not care about her health.

cont.

96

Activity 2. Judgement of eating with regards to weight or size

In this activity, compare what you perceive as *healthy* or *unhealthy eating* within the same categories as in Activity 1. I've created two tables for this activity: one for what you perceive as healthy and one for what you perceive as unhealthy eating. Again, you can fill them in your Workbook or draw these up in your journal. You may find it useful to take some time eating in a variety of different environments, with different people around you, for all your perceptions to fully arise, along with the judgements of others.

cont.

Eating *Healthily*

	Judgement of **self**	My judgement of **others**	How I think others judge **me**
Desirable weight or Size	e.g. I'm so good. e.g. I'm proud of myself. e.g. I'm in control of my eating.	e.g. They have great discipline.	e.g. She's so dedicated to her health. e.g. I'm acceptable.
Undesirable Weight or Size	e.g. I'm so good. e.g. It's so unfair, I eat like a rabbit and still look like a blimp. e.g. Why can't I eat like this all the time?	e.g. How unlucky is she that she eats healthily and yet has an unhealthy weight. e.g. At least she's trying.	e.g. She probably just eats like this when she's out in public. e.g. Maybe she should try exercise as well.

cont.

98

Eating *Unhealthily*		
Judgement of self	**My judgement of others**	**How I think others judge me**
e.g. I've blown all the hard work of my diet. I'm useless. e.g. A treat now and then is okay, but make sure you don't let this get out of hand.	e.g. She's so lucky to be able to eat like that and maintain a healthy weight. e.g. I feel angry that other people don't have to worry about their weight.	e.g. She'd better not eat like that frequently, or before she knows it, she'll blow up like a balloon.
Judgement of self	**My judgement of others**	**How I think others judge me**
e.g. I've absolutely no self-control. e.g. I'm so ashamed of my eating.	e.g. She's got no self-control. e.g. Does she not care about her body? e.g. No wonder she's overweight if she eats like that.	e.g. She's got no self-respect or dignity. e.g. She's disgusting. e.g. Does she not know of the health risks of obesity (implying stupidity).

Desirable weight or Size ... *Undesirable Weight or Size*

cont.

Reflection

On completing these tables, take the time to consider whether you fear the judgement of being your current weight or size. Whether you fear the judgement of eating a specific way? Whether you fear judgement when you eat healthily or unhealthily? Whether you fear judgement if you were to lose or gain weight? Whether you fear judgement no matter your size? Whether you judge others in larger bodies or those that have what you would consider a desirable weight?

Consider whether your judgements or fear of judgement contradict one another. You may see where you have conflicting perspectives, and potentially, how you fear or are judgemental of the very thing you desire. It makes sense that you could possibly sabotage your weight loss efforts if you label individuals with a desirable body as self-centred, superficial or attention-seeking, as you may not want to be judged or perceived this way yourself.

Reflect on how your judgement of others may impact your perception of yourself, and record how you felt about this activity in your Workbook or journal.

Reclaim Confidence

If you believe that others judge you for being overweight or unhealthy, it can lead you to conclude that you'll feel more confident when you achieve your ideal weight or health goals. Yet how much weight do you need to lose to feel confident? And is being your goal weight a sure-fire way to confidence?

The thing is, you don't achieve confidence when you attain a certain weight, dress size, or any other external goal. Confidence arises when you release your fear of judgement; of concerning yourself with what other people think of you… when you can be unapologetically you.

Confidence is only a perception anyway; it doesn't exist in absolute terms. Confidence is perceived through the manner in which someone conducts themselves. It's possible to perceive someone as confident, when in fact they are uncertain and unsure of themselves. Conversely, someone who is knowledgeable and experienced in a subject may appear timid and uncertain, and not at all confident. In this way, confidence is a perception determined by someone's self-assuredness and preparedness to take chances in a specific situation.

Confidence is accessible to you right now through releasing the fear of being judged and attempting to meet others' expectations, without you having to change anything.

What You Weigh Does Not Define You

Despite what you've been led to believe, your weight, body, health, sexual orientation or ethnicity don't define who you are, or dictate your value as a person. And most definitely, your identity is not locked up in your physical appearance.

The perception that your weight or body provides insight into who you are is illogical: you don't choose your body in the same way that you would choose clothing or jewellery. Your body is not a reflection of who you are. It is the vehicle that enables you to enjoy your life: to experience and interact with the world around you.

Not only does your body not define who you are, but your perception of yourself and your body may be distorted. A distorted self-perception is especially an issue for individuals with eating disorders. Yet, it seems that most people don't see their body as it truly is. A study of 1,932 adolescents' perception of their weight found that girls of a healthy weight considered themselves overweight, and as a consequence adopted dieting behaviour in response to their weight perception, not their actual weight (59).

You are Enough

Employing self-criticism, dissatisfaction and self-loathing as motivators for weight loss or health improvement often backfire. This is because they're founded on the belief that you're not worthy of success and happiness. Unfortunately, weight loss will not resolve these feelings of self-loathing. Weight loss may quieten your *inner critic* for a while. However, your inner critic will continue to nag at you, regardless of your weight, until you resolve the false perception that you are not worthy of contentment or good enough. It is not your weight or your health that needs to change, but the thoughts that you are not good enough or worthy of happiness or success as you are right now.

You may have had an experience when someone said something negative and you brushed it off or even thought, *I'll prove you wrong.* I know I did. My Year 11 chemistry teacher, who told me I should switch subjects as I apparently didn't have the aptitude for chemistry. I wanted to study science at university and was defiant in my thoughts: *I am good enough, and I am going to prove you wrong.* I recruited a chemistry tutor and studied consistently. By the following semester, I'd received top grades in the chemistry class. This was a time when I didn't believe the story that I wasn't good enough and would never make it.

Although there may be times you rise above self-doubt or the doubt that others express in you, there may be other times when someone says you aren't good enough and it causes you to shatter inside. Or nobody said anything at all, yet you felt like a failure: you didn't get the job; you didn't get a call after the date; the phone isn't ringing off the hook with inquiries for your services. The reason these comments or circumstances hurt is because you fear that maybe you aren't good enough: *he's right, what hope do I ever have at excelling at chemistry? Why bother, my efforts won't amount to anything anyway. I've tried everything; it's too hard.* The list is exhaustive: *I'm not skilled enough, talented enough, knowledgeable enough, pretty enough, smart enough, funny enough, engaging enough,* and so on.

It is your mind that creates the thoughts in order to explain someone's actions or your circumstances. However, these thoughts are only stories your mind makes up. They are not the absolute truth. If someone or something makes you feel like you're not good enough, it is because on some level you believe what they're saying. Why is this?

Your belief system is like a filter through which you interpret everything that happens in your life. It influences what you pay attention to and how you experience the world. If you feel that everyone is talking about weight loss and everywhere you look there are blogs, posts and articles on healthy eating and weight loss, understand that it is your belief system, through which you perceive the world, that makes it appear this way. It's like when you buy a specific make and model of car and then start to notice them everywhere. This make and model of car was always there. It's just that now your brain is more aware of them as it has relevance to you. When you end your preoccupation with weight and body image, it can feel like the whole world has too.

The thing is, you are neither worthy nor unworthy, deserving nor undeserving, enough nor not enough: you just are. Who you are is not defined by your appearance or actions. In one situation you may have made an incredibly *smart* move, and in that moment, you consider yourself as *smart*. In another moment you may make a decision that's incredibly *stupid*, and in that moment, you consider yourself as *stupid*. The first consequence of thinking this way is that you interpret your decisions or actions as either smart or stupid—positive or negative. The second consequence is that you label yourself as either smart or stupid, depending on your interpretation of the situation. However, you are neither smart nor stupid. Your perception of yourself as one or the other is dependent on the situation and is not absolute.

You are neither smart nor stupid, pretty nor ugly, selfless nor selfish, confident nor timid, forgetful nor attentive, hard-working nor lazy, caring nor uncaring. Only when you judge yourself and identify with these labels, do you perceive yourself as one or the other. If you hold onto identifying yourself by these opposites, you'll find that you constantly switch your self-perception from one to the other. When you perceive that you are selfish, you may feel immense guilt and reprimand yourself. When you perceive yourself as selfless, you may feel a sense of pride and self-worth.

Similar to the two sides of one coin, when you identify as selfless, the other side of the coin, selfish, continues to exist. As a consequence, you can end up spending your entire life flipping from one thought to the other: *I am selfish, I am selfless, I am selfish*, on and on the thoughts go. However, you are neither. It is only the mental labelling based on your perception of your behaviours and circumstances that cause you to believe that you are one or the other.

An unfortunate consequence of not feeling worthy is that you can spend your entire life trying to be a better version of yourself. But that is not inherently the problem. The problem is that you can deprive yourself of self-acceptance and self-care until some arbitrary point in time that never arises. All when you are worthy of self-acceptance and self-care as you are, right now, since your weight does not reflect your self-worth.

Who You Are

"What a liberation to realize that the "voice in my head" is not who I am."

– Eckhart Tolle, *New Earth*

When you believe thoughts such as, *I'll only be good enough when I lose weight*, or *I'll only be worthy of happiness and contentment when my body meets society's standards*, you are attaching your self-worth to your physical body. However, as previously mentioned, you don't choose or control your body. Nor does your body indicate who you are as a person. Your body is not who you are. You are the witness, aware of your body through your five senses: sight, sound, smell, taste and touch.

Thoughts arise in your mind that interpret, categorise and judge your body, people and situations. Yet these thoughts arise without your control. You also don't control your past experiences, natural propensity and personality, all which influence how you perceive the world. Therefore, you are not your thoughts, but the witness aware of the thoughts that arise.

When you realise that you are the witness of *what is*, you can let go of the thoughts that your body has somehow betrayed you or that you need to control it. There is nothing you need to change, achieve or attain, to be worthy of experiencing the aliveness of who you are right now.

This does not imply that you shouldn't take action to nourish and nurture your body. But that rather than imposing rules on yourself or attempting to control your body, notice how different foods, body movements, thoughts and attitudes make you feel. And thus, take action in a more inquisitive and intuitive way.

Let Go of Perfectionism

"Perfectionism is a self destructive and addictive belief system that fuels this primary thought: If I look perfect, and do everything perfectly, I can avoid or minimise the painful feelings of shame, judgement, and blame."

—Brené Brown.

Diets encourage you to look for fault in yourself, so that you continually desire to improve or perfect yourself. In regards to dieting, you may perceive perfection as following the diet rules exactly, achieving the desired results, or meeting societal standards of beauty.

However, perfection does not exist in absolute terms. Perfectionism is founded on the belief that there is a right or wrong way to be or to do something. But there is no absolute right or wrong. You are unique, and what will work for you to achieve success and happiness will differ from what will work for someone else. As I've said before, perfectly following a diet, plan or strategy provides no guarantee of success for you.

Further, the rules, expectations and standards will keep changing, whether as a result of changing society standards, changes in your own perception, or as we gain improved knowledge and understanding of the human body. Therefore, aspiring for perfection is like trying to obtain the pot of gold at the end of a rainbow. No matter how close—perfect—you get, it seems to move just a little further out of reach as the goal posts keep moving, or you find yourself striving for another goal.

Even if perfection were possible, you could not be perfect all of the time. Life happens. There will always be days where things don't go according to plan.

Striving for perfection can even hinder your progress because the desire to achieve perfection can lead to an *all-or-nothing* mindset: where you either do a diet or follow a plan or strategy perfectly or not at all. The immense pressure to succeed can cause you to believe that it is better *not to act* than take action and fail. The all-or-nothing mindset can become a form of resistance, so that you put off change until you've found the *right approach* or are certain that you can attain results. You may even at times use food as a way to rebel against the endless pursuit of perfection. Thus, sabotaging your efforts.

When you recognise that there is no right or wrong way to approach your diet and that each person can forge their own unique path to feel healthy and happy, it becomes possible for you to release the reins of control. You can then acknowledge that you don't need to be perfect to be good enough, worthy or deserving of being alive, loved, happy and content.

Let's explore an alternative approach to honouring your body—to nurture and nourish it—just as it is right now.

Joyful Eating Principle 2.
ACCEPT YOUR BODY

In this moment, your body is exactly the weight, size and shape it should be. No amount of resisting *what is*, blame or guilt will change your body in this moment. Accept the body you have right now, and choose to move, nourish and care for it in ways that make you feel most energetic and alive. Let go of controlling and punishing yourself for *what is* in this moment.

PART II

Implementing the Practice of Joyful Eating

9

Get Curious About Why You Eat

"Be curious, not judgemental."

— Walt Whitman

You eat to acquire energy and nourishment, right? Well, this is a yes and no answer. Although it's true that your body signals that it is hungry, it is your mind that decides whether or not you eat, and what you choose to eat. Further, the reasons you eat go far beyond physical hunger. It is possible for your mind to create an appetite for food in response to exposure to food, to thinking about food, or to your emotional state, in the complete absence of physical hunger. Hence, casually walking past a pizzeria may cause you to salivate and feel pangs of hunger, orient you towards eating pizza or influence what you prepare for dinner. So, your eating behaviour and food choices are associated with much more than a need for physical nourishment. Let's explore some common reasons for eating.

Common Reasons for Eating

Hunger

Hunger is a true physical sensation signalling to your body that you require nourishment.

Habit

Habitual eating occurs when you eat without conscious thought or acknowledgement that you are hungry. It's heading to the fridge as soon as you get home, grabbing a snack at the counter of a petrol station simply because they're there, or nibbling on nuts, chips or lollies from a bowl or bag without even realising you're doing it. Habitual eating occurs when you eat on autopilot, often without an awareness of the experience of eating.

Learned behaviour

Learned behaviours are similar to habits in that they can seem automatic and don't necessarily involve conscious thought. Yet, learned behaviours are formed from beliefs and habits picked up from others throughout your life.

Learned behaviours may include things you've been told directly, such as 'clean your plate' or 'eat all your vegetables, and then you can have dessert'. Other learned behaviours may have been reinforced through observation, or eating in specific situations or moods. For example, I had a client who didn't particularly enjoy chocolate. However, when she felt she needed to *escape* or have quiet time to herself, she would eat chocolate. On reflection, she recalled as a child that this is what her mother would do after an argument with her father. She had adopted a learnt behaviour.

Environmental cues

The way your environment is set up, and the subsequent effects on your eating behaviour and choices, has been written about extensively in books and the scientific literature. There are numerous theories and examples of how your environment influences your eating, such as how having easy access to food can increase your consumption of it, or how the shape and size of your glasses and plates can affect your perception of portion size, and thus how much you eat (61). I'm not suggesting that you attempt to *fool* yourself to eat less by decreasing the size of your plate or the height of your glass, but become aware of the environmental cues that might cause you to eat and influence your food choices and the quantities you eat.

Environmental cues are important, as seeing food can lead to eating or a desire to eat. You may not have felt hungry until food was offered to you or you passed a café. I've heard people respond to the question 'are you hungry?' with, 'I could eat'. Or they may respond 'no' and then change their mind once they see what's on offer. It's what's been colloquially termed the *see-food diet*: you see food, you eat food.

Associations

Sometimes you may associate eating with certain activities, times of the day or behaviours. You may relate to some of these food and activity associations:

- eating when kids get home from school
- supper when kids have gone to bed (even when you've already had dinner)
- treats after breakups or arguments
- chips or snacks with watching TV
- fish and chips with being at the beach
- lollies with long drives or trips
- popcorn with a movie
- a biscuit (or two) with a cup of tea
- a glass of wine on getting home from work

You may find that you have very specific associations based on your past conditioning and experiences. There was a time when I associated going to the library with eating cake, as the library was close to a coffee shop I enjoyed visiting. Enjoying a visit to the library and a cake afterwards is a great experience, but when it became a habit and I'd head for the cake even if I wasn't hungry, I started to see that this association was causing me to eat despite no physical hunger. I didn't stop this behaviour outright, but instead asked myself before I progressed to the coffee shop, *am I truly hungry in this moment?* If the answer were no, I'd head back home or enjoy my new book under a tree. Thus, I formed a new habit.

Eating Rules

Eating rules are rules for *what, when* and *how* you eat. You may have formed these rules yourself or have had them imposed on you by diets or other external influences. An eating rule may be eating to the clock: eating because it is breakfast time, lunch time or dinner time.

You may eat because it's time for a work break, or because you perceive it as unhealthy to skip a meal. You may eat quantities to compensate for previous under- or overeating or exercise. Or because you are concerned about what others will think of you if you don't join them in a meal or celebratory dish. You may eat or drink because there is still liquid in the bottle, food left in the package or on your plate.

Emotions

Eating for emotional reasons is a common human behaviour. Eating to celebrate. Eating because you are proud, happy, sad, bored or lonely. Sometimes this is okay, but emotional eating can become a problem when it's your most common reason for eating or when it leads to uncontrollable eating or overeating in order to numb out or to amplify positive, or even negative, emotions.

✑ Why you choose to eat

Take the time to explore your physical and non-physical reasons for eating (or not eating), and record them in your Workbook or journal. You may find that reasons come to mind immediately. If not, you may find it helpful to reflect on your reasons for eating for a few days, up to a week.

Some of the reasons that may come to mind include:

- hunger
- nourishment
- energy
- it's time to eat
- habit
- distraction
- indecisiveness
- stress
- comfort
- pleasure
- sweetness
- craving
- entertainment
- escape

- rebellion
- self-soothing
- avoidance
- numbness
- association
- food is available
- convenience
- connection
- celebration
- reward
- cheering yourself up
- loneliness
- emotions

- familiarity
- security
- meaning
- overwhelm
- boredom
- fear of judgement
- to feel (inflict) pain
- to reinforce the belief that you are *bad* or *unlovable*
- guilt and shame

The purpose of this activity is not to control or change your eating in any way, but to become aware of the cues and behaviours that influence your eating. Reflect on which of your reasons for eating are hunger, habit, learned behaviours, environmental cues, associations, eating rules or emotions.

Through an awareness of your primary reasons for eating, you could establish questions to ask yourself when you are deciding whether to eat or not. These questions could be:

- Why am I eating (or not eating)?
- Am I physically hungry?

cont.

117

- Am I eating out of habit?

- Am I eating on autopilot?

- Am I eating in response to external cues?

- Am I eating to comply with social norms or to make my eating companions feel comfortable?

- Am I eating this food because I perceive it as healthy or unhealthy, good or bad?

- Am I eating because of the rules that I (or society as a whole) have around eating and this food, such as time of day, what constitutes a meal, portions etc.?

- Am I fulfilling emotional needs? What are the emotions that lead me to eat?

In your Workbook or journal, you may like to record one or two specific questions you would like to consider before eating for the next week or ongoing. I recommend focusing on only one or two questions each week, so as not to overwhelm yourself and so that each time you eat it is not an internal interrogation.

Keep a Food and Mood Journal

Keeping a Food and Mood Journal can be helpful to identify the emotions and thoughts that cause you to eat when you are not hungry. Thus, enabling you to change your food choices and eating behaviour. For example, if you discover that your eating is more in response to emotional reasons, you could then begin to explore other ways to deal with your emotions or seek help.

The important thing is not to reprimand yourself if you know you're eating purely for emotional reasons and can't seem to stop yourself. In the *heat of the moment,* when your emotions are too intense to deal with, it can be difficult to swerve away from the compulsion to eat, and that's okay. To start, simply be aware of this behaviour and take note of why you feel this way.

You may also begin to uncover the thoughts that underlie your behaviours and emotions. For example, if you find yourself stopping at a service station to buy a snack and then feel guilty, you can notice the associated thoughts, such as, *I should never have eaten this*; *I have no self-control*; *I am never going to lose this weight.*

Accept *what is*: you have bought and have consumed the snack. You cannot change what has already happened through guilt or self-reprimanding. Instead of guilting yourself, use this as an opportunity to identify the thoughts associated with the emotions before, during and after you eat.

✍ How to keep a Food and Mood Journal

In your Workbook or journal, record when, what and how much (and how quickly) you ate, and how you felt emotionally and physically before, during and after eating. Note any thoughts or feelings about your eating or circumstances at the time of eating, which may have impacted your emotions or reason for eating. I recommend keeping a Food and Mood Journal for at least one week to enable you to see patterns in your eating. Include:

- meals and snacks
- beverages, including alcohol
- cigarettes
- chewing gum or lollies

Below I've included a list of moods/emotions and physical sensations, to help you characterise how you are feeling. Different intensities of similar emotions are grouped together to make it easier for you to pick the emotion that you are feeling.

You may choose to write in your Workbook or journal at every meal or once a day. How much detail you record is up to you; it may depend on the time you have available or what aspect of your eating you want to explore.

cont.

If accounting for your every mouthful has been a dieting activity that has led you to anxiety and stress previously, perhaps keep the details and quantities of what you eat vague, and instead focus on your mood and the physical sensations in your body. You may prefer not to record quantities at all and focus solely on what and why you ate (or did not eat).

Moods and Emotions

happy	tired	lazy	frantic	guilty
content	fatigued	unhappy	uncomfortable	mortified
calm	exhausted	disappointed	awkward	frightened
relaxed	drained	dissatisfied	nervous	concerned
cheerful	sleepy	upset	worried	bothered
fulfilled	rundown	depressed	embarrassed	frustrated
pleased	bored	offended	humiliated	irritated
excited	fed up	hurt	panicky	annoyed
energetic	restless	tense	anxious	angry
proud	lethargic	stressed	ashamed	furious

Physical Sensations

starving	shaky	reflux	burping	sleepy
famished	dizzy	painful	bloated	lethargic
hungry	faint	spasms	bowel motion	tired
satisfied	queasy	gurgling	constipated	energetic
full	nauseous	sore	diarrhoea	
stuffed	vomiting	heartburn	jittery	
lightheaded	cramped	flatulence	racing	

Remember not to judge what or how much you did or did not eat, whether the food is good or bad, or whether you should or should not have eaten it. This is not an exercise in disciplining or reprimanding yourself, but rather observing your food choices and eating behaviour.

cont.

You may like to note the thoughts that arise in your Workbook or journal, observing them without attachment, analysis or resistance.

Keep a Food and Mood Journal for as long as you find helpful. Do it every so often, as your relationship with food is not static, but constantly changing.

10

Eat with Your Full Awareness

"Most humans are never fully present in the now, because unconsciously they believe that the next moment must be more important than this one. But then you miss your whole life, which is never not now."

— Eckhart Tolle

Picture this: you arrive home after work, hungry and tired. It feels too hard to prepare something healthy, so you fill up on quick and easy pre-packaged food, a takeaway or the usual boring meal you have most evenings. You eat semi-consciously, distracted, in front of the TV. Or perhaps you eat out of a container or standing in the kitchen, because you have so many chores or caretaking to do. You then find yourself desiring a snack, treat or drink to help relax and unwind. The next day, you may mindlessly eat as you rush out the door for work or school, grabbing a bite to eat to tide you over, sometimes skipping breakfast altogether. Later, you perhaps eat lunch at your desk or in a hurry between meetings or clients. To then snack at your desk or consume foods simply because they're on offer in the tearoom or you need the distraction from your work.

Distracted and unconscious eating is not only commonplace, it is almost revered in the same way that being busy is revered. However, neither mindless eating nor being *busy* the majority of the time beneficial to your

122

body or your relationship to food. In an unconscious or distracted state, you might eat while your body is in the stress response, thus influencing your digestion and assimilation of nutrients (62). So, you are less likely aware of your body's hunger signals and responses to the type and volume of food you eat. More importantly, you might not experience the full pleasure and sensory experience of what you eat.

On the other hand, an awareness that you are eating stimulates digestion through messages between your brain and gastrointestinal tract, known as the cephalic phase of digestion (63). The sight of food stimulates the release of saliva, stomach acid, and digestive enzymes to prepare for the breakdown of food. The smell of food amplifies this. Then, as you taste food, the taste receptors prepare your digestive system for the food to come, plus the type of food. So that for example, sugary food stimulates digestive enzymes that break down sugars. These responses are further enhanced by the act of chewing and swallowing food. Not only this, an awareness that you're eating has actually been shown to promote the secretion of the blood sugar regulating hormone insulin, even before glucose (sugar) levels in the bloodstream rise (64,65). Therefore, engaging your senses in eating not only influences your digestion but also how your body utilises and responds to the nutrition provided.

Furthermore, when you eat with your full awareness, you may notice that the speed at which you eat naturally slows. This natural slowing of eating may help to increase fullness and reduce energy intake. In contrast, eating quickly is associated with reduced satiety, increased body weight and insulin resistance (66,67,68,69,70). Despite these possible consequences, the intent is not to slow, reduce or control your eating, it is to eat with your full awareness.

Conscious Eating

I call the drawing of your full awareness to *what* and *why* you are eating, *conscious eating*. I use the term *conscious* rather than mindful because the term *mindful eating* can be misinterpreted and has been hijacked by the diet industry. Some diet proponents use mindful eating practices for weight loss, although mindful eating is not a weight loss tool. And some people use the term *mindful* to infer a degree of control; they may state, 'I am mindful of what I eat', inferring that they only eat healthy food or are mindful not to eat *too* much.

In other instances, mindfulness is considered a meditation practice, and with this comes a perception that there is a right or wrong way to practise it. I've experienced mindfulness meditation classes where I've been told how to sit, breathe and be. Yet, there is no right or wrong way to eat with your full awareness. Furthermore, some people may associate mindfulness with religious or devotional practices.

Since many of the aspects of mindful eating, such as non-judgement, no control, and self-compassion, are covered elsewhere in this book, the practice introduced here is more appropriately termed *conscious eating*. Let's explore the practice of conscious eating.

The practice of conscious eating reminds me of the scene in the movie, *City of Angels*, where Seth (Nicolas Cage) is an angel who has no sense of taste or feel. He asks Meg Ryan's character, Maggie Rice, to describe how a pear tastes. At first, she is a little embarrassed by the question and then answers, 'it tastes like a pear'. 'But I want to know what a pear tastes like to you?', Seth asks. To this, she replies, 'it is sweet, juicy and grainy'.

Like Meg Ryan's character, you may have disengaged your senses and curiosity when eating. To eat consciously, engaging all your senses, is completely natural and instinctive. But, like Maggie Rice, you may require a little coaxing to reignite this innate ability.

Eat Without Distraction

Conscious eating is eating with your full awareness, without distraction. If you're busy, you may feel you have too much to juggle to do nothing but eat, and so multi-task your eating. You are not alone. Just walk into a café and you'll witness a considerable portion of patrons drinking coffee and eating with their eyes glued to their phone or laptop. Despite this multi-tasking appearing to be productive, this distraction means that you are not fully engaging your senses in the process of eating… and possibly not with your work either!

Another common reason for eating with a distraction is that you may feel uncomfortable doing nothing but eat, especially if you're at work or at a café alone. You may feel uncomfortable with what the other patrons or your colleagues will think of you if you're sitting enjoying a meal without anything to occupy your eyes. You may believe that it's better to look busy, popular, important or distracted than to look like a *loner* or to engage with others.

The resistance to doing nothing but eat may not only relate to what others think of you; you may feel uncomfortable having time alone with your thoughts. I've had clients say that they have so much going on in their lives that they fear if they stop, they will break down and not be able to continue with all their responsibilities.

Feeling overwhelmed by your responsibilities can be challenging, yet ignoring your body, thoughts and emotions does more to fuel this exasperated feeling than dissolve it. I'm not suggesting that slowing down and eating undistracted will resolve all your issues. However, this one practice may have flow-on effects to other aspects of your life. It may reduce your feeling of stress, improve your digestion, and increase your enjoyment and satisfaction in what you eat.

Another resistance to conscious eating may be that an awareness of your eating could diminish the numbing influence of food over your emotions. As a consequence, you may become more aware of your emotions and you are unsure you can deal with them. If you can relate, you may need more time before practising conscious eating. Alternatively, you may find it beneficial to seek emotional support. Accept that where you are right now is exactly where you are meant to be, and then consider the next steps to take.

Take the Time to Eat

If you're eating three or more times a day and drinking a few beverages, you have numerous opportunities every day to practise conscious eating. Conscious eating can be an alternative to other mindfulness practices, as you can practise conscious eating without requiring additional time or effort.

You may find that you often eat distractedly or quickly because you are focused on the next thing to do. However, taking a break away from your desk or responsibilities, even for 5-15 minutes, can enable you to relax your body, quieten your mind and gain some perspective. Thus, it allows you to return to your tasks with a clearer mind. Taking a break can potentially increase your productivity rather than decrease it, which is often the concern people have with taking time out to eat or relax. When you eat, there is nothing else for you to do but eat. When you move on to the next task, do so with your full attention.

If you're concerned about the amount of time required to begin a practice of conscious eating, know that you don't have to practise conscious eating with every meal. You could begin by eating just one meal a day or week with your full awareness. Alternatively, you could start with your favourite food; a food that you perceive as a *guilty pleasure* or that you frequently eat distractedly, such as in front of the TV or at your desk.

How to Consciously Eat a Doughnut

Once you've decided what and when to eat, for example, a cinnamon doughnut, eat with your full awareness of the sensory experience of eating. Bring your entire awareness to how the doughnut looks. Inhale, and notice how it smells. Bite into it and notice how it feels. Notice the fluffy white centre in contrast to the golden-brown outer layer. Notice the softness of the spongy centre as contrasted to the oily outside. Notice the crunch of sugar between your teeth and its graininess against your lips. Feel the sugar dissolve in your mouth, on your tongue, and as you chew. Notice the change in texture and the sounds as you bite, chew, and swallow each mouthful. Taste the sweetness of sugar and the aromatic flavour of cinnamon. Notice how the flavours change as the sugar, cinnamon and doughy centre combine through your chewing. Take the time to savour the flavours that linger in your mouth once you've swallowed each mouthful: savour every mouthful.

Maintain your awareness on all the sensory inputs of eating, and continue to eat the doughnut until you are either full or no longer enjoy it. There is no rule that once you've started eating a doughnut, you have to eat it all.

You may find that the taste sensation dissipates; in this case, stop eating as it no longer brings you pleasure. You may discover that you don't enjoy doughnuts as much as you believed you did, or that it doesn't feel good in your body. Or you may discover you truly love doughnuts and relish every mouthful.

✍ Practise conscious eating

Sit somewhere with little distraction to eat your meal or snack. Do one thing at a time: eat, rather than drive, work at your desk, worry over an issue, or stand at the kitchen counter or refrigerator.

Place your food on a plate or in a bowl, where you can observe the colours, shapes and textures. Observe the physical sensations in your body and your desire to eat. Are you hungry? Or are you simply tempted by what's in front of you? Do you sense a physical or emotional desire to eat?

Decide whether or not to eat. If you choose to eat, do so consciously aware of all your senses.

Take a deep inhale to experience the aroma of the food.

Take a bite, and tune into the senses of sound, taste and feel.

Chew the food slowly, noticing how the sound, smell, taste and texture changes as you chew. Notice the sounds and sensations as you swallow.

Keep your full awareness on eating for the entire meal, noticing if the sensations dull or intensify as you carry on eating. Continue to eat if you're still hungry and the food is bringing you pleasure. Stop eating once you feel full or are no longer enjoying the food.

Observe whether there is a temptation to take the next bite before you've finished chewing your previous mouthful. Consider whether you're anticipating the next mouthful without fully enjoying the one you're eating.

Once you've finished eating, notice how the food feels in your body. After the meal, draw your awareness from time to time to how it made you feel physically and emotionally. You may note in your Workbook or journal how it felt to eat consciously, and what you noticed about your enjoyment of the food or your eating behaviour. Also, note whether you felt any resistance to doing nothing but eat.

Continuing the Practice of Conscious Eating

To begin with, you may try to consciously eat a few meals during the week or all your meals for one day. As you continue to practise conscious eating, you may find that it becomes more automatic. However, don't *beat yourself up* if at times you forget to eat consciously, desire to eat in front of the TV, or eat fast without noticing that you've eaten. In these instances, notice that you've eaten mindlessly. Then, try to practise conscious eating with your next meal or snack. Even when it becomes quite automatic to eat consciously, you may find it useful to intentionally practise conscious eating one day or one meal a week, to reinforce the behaviour of conscious eating.

Even if you're eating in company, at a meeting, or you have no choice but to eat at your desk, you can still bring your awareness to eating. You don't necessarily need to step away from your desk to bring your full attention to eating. In any environment, with anyone around you, you can engage all your senses as you eat and draw your attention away from distractions.

Each time that you eat, you don't necessarily have to focus on all the senses at once. Another approach is to focus on one sense with a meal or beverage. Thus, a single meal or beverage may have one of the below focuses:

Sight

Focus on how your meal or snack looks. Notice the colours, shapes, textures, and shadows. You may focus solely on the food in front of you, or incorporate observing objects surrounding you, and then bring your attention back to your meal. Do so without labelling the food or objects in your surroundings as either good or bad; simply witness *what is.*

Sound

Observe the sounds in your environment: the sounds of your utensils gathering food, of your biting into, chewing and swallowing the food. You may move your attention from one sound to another; from those that are close, such as your breath or the sounds made by your teeth and jaw as you chew, to sounds off in the distance, such as noises created by a breeze, bird calls or distant traffic.

Feel

Focus on physical sensations such as the texture of fabric or air movement on your skin. Feel the food as you bite into it and notice the sensations in your jaw as you chew, and of the food between your teeth. Draw your awareness to how the texture of food changes as you chew, and how it feels as you swallow. You may notice the feeling in your throat and abdomen, and notice how the sensations of hunger give way to fullness.

Smell

Notice aromas in your surroundings by taking a few deep breaths before you begin to eat. Bring the food to your nose and take a deep inhale. Take in the aroma of the meal before you eat. Notice how the smell changes as you continue to eat. If the sense of smell dissipates, you may like to continue your meal by focusing on your breath: following your inhale and exhale.

Taste

Another time you may focus on taste, noticing how the taste changes with each mouthful and as you chew. This can be particularly effective if you're eating a salad or other mix, where each mouthful is likely to give you a slightly different combination of ingredients. Notice how the taste changes as you chew and that remains in your mouth after you swallow. Notice if the taste intensifies or whether the level of enjoyment dissipates as you take more mouthfuls.

Cautiously Engage the Sense of Sight

The first sense you engage when you eat is that of sight. Although, at the sight of food, you might immediately attach different stories and beliefs without truly tasting and experiencing it. I became deeply aware of this when I experienced dining in the dark. In the pitch black, I was unaware of what I was eating and had to rely on my other senses—that of smell, feel, sound and taste. I enjoyed the taste and sensations of foods that I wouldn't normally choose, due to preconceptions of my preferences. Therefore, it is important to focus on the sense of sight—that is, its colours, shapes and textures—not the labels and thoughts you have attached to what you are eating.

Observing the food you are eating can also provide an awareness of the quantity you're consuming. This can better enable you to adjust your eating based on your body's responses. For example, if you can see exactly how much sugar is going into your morning latte, you're in a better position to adjust it, and determine the portion that tastes and feels best to your body. If you place chips or M&Ms into a bowl, you're better able to gauge with your eyes what you feel an appropriate portion is for you the next time you choose to enjoy this same food. The intent is not to control your portion sizes, but to be aware of what and how you're eating. Through this observation, you may vary your portion sizes or the variety on your plate based on what looks appealing, not on diet rules or an attempt to control your calorie intake.

Most of the time, I no longer eat corn chips straight from the bag as I used to, but place what I feel will satisfy me into a bowl. If the amount in the bowl doesn't satisfy me, I tune in to my body to determine whether I am hungrier than I thought, or whether I simply want them because they're there and delicious. Before reaching for a second bowl, I tune into my body to determine whether I'd like more chips, or whether I may require a small meal instead. If I'm not hungry—I just wanted the chips because they're there—I can then investigate the thoughts and emotions that contribute to this behaviour, rather than mindlessly grabbing another bowlful of chips.

Through eating consciously, and applying it to various foods and situations, I've begun to realise how much our preconceived beliefs about food can prevent us from tasting and experiencing the food we eat. When your eating is clouded by thoughts of what you like or dislike, what is healthy or not healthy, it can influence your enjoyment.

Conscious Eating Connects You with the Now

The intention of conscious eating is to be fully present with the act of eating, without thought of what you should or should not be eating. It is an act of being fully present in the now.

It can seem that the concept of *living in the now* would imply there is no care of tomorrow and would promote eating without consideration of future consequences. However, *being in the now*, is about connection and awareness of your body in this moment; with an awareness of how the food you eat feels in your body and how your body responds to it.

When you believe that you shouldn't enjoy a food now due to future consequences, you're taking yourself out of the present moment. When you focus on external rules and cues, it can cause you to eat more or less than your body requires, causing an imbalance in your energy intake. It is this imbalance which can lead you to believe that your body can't be trusted. Next, let's explore your hunger cues and how you can learn to listen to and trust your hunger.

Joyful Eating Principle 3.
CONSCIOUSLY EAT

Eat without distractions, drawing your full awareness to the sensory experience of sight, smell, taste, sound and feel, without judgement or mental commentary.

Eating with your full attention can relax your body, quieten your mind, reduce stress, improve digestion and increase satisfaction.

11

Respect Your Hunger

*"Your relationship to food, no matter how
conflicted, is the doorway to freedom."*

— Geneen Roth

Hunger is a physical sensation that occurs when your stomach and body signal to your brain that energy and nourishment is required. It is an instinctive signal to eat.

Except, dieting can ruin all that. It is possible that you distrust or fear hunger, or your response to hunger, as a consequence of dieting. This is because diets often require you to ignore or override your hunger signals, which can result in an intensification of hunger and what you may consider uncontrollable eating or overeating. Hence, dieting reinforces the perception that you cannot trust your hunger signals.

Appetite, on the other hand, is a desire for food that originates from thought. You can be hungry but have no desire to eat, and thus have no appetite. Alternatively, you can have an appetite for food when there is no physical hunger. This disparity between hunger and appetite may occur, for example, when you're hungry but too emotional to eat, or when you're offered delicious food and eat despite no prior physical hunger. Appetite is a learnt behaviour, driven by past conditioning and preferences. You develop an appetite for food, not in response to hunger but because you enjoy it, have restricted it in the past, or perceive it as *naughty*.

Although appetite originates from thought, it can create changes in your body to prepare it for food, and can subsequently stimulate physical sensations of hunger. Just thinking about food can increase saliva production, release gastric juices and digestive enzymes, and thus create grumbling in your stomach (71). You may have experienced this at times when you were not physically hungry, but then you saw or smelt some tempting food, and suddenly felt hungry. The cake is mouth-watering, literally!

No matter whether the impulse to eat is hunger or appetite; ultimately it is your brain that decides whether or not you eat and what you'll eat. So, when your brain receives a signal that you are hungry or desire a food, a stream of thoughts follows: *I feel hungry, what should I eat? I can't believe I'm already hungry, I only ate an hour ago. How am I ever going to lose these excess kilos? I really need to stick to that meal plan. I didn't prepare an afternoon snack anyway. Oh, there is leftover cake in the staff fridge. It was so good. No, I shouldn't eat it. I should have a piece of fruit or a cup of tea; don't they say that sometimes when you believe you're hungry, you're actually thirsty? But the cake is there, and I don't have cake that often. What difference is one piece of cake going to make anyway? If I eat it now, I'll be good for the rest of this week.*

It is your thoughts that cause you to either eat or forgo the cake. And unfortunately, eating the cake is not a sure-fire way to quieten your mind. Eating the cake is likely to be followed by another stream of thoughts such as, *I feel so full. I really shouldn't have eaten that cake. I can't believe I let myself eat it. I'm so weak. I'm pathetic. How am I ever going to lose this excess weight? I'll have to work out harder this evening. Should I skip breakfast tomorrow?*

The thing is, it's not that physical hunger or your appetite is good or bad, but that your thoughts about hunger and your response to it make it so. Your entire life you have been exposed to *rules* around hunger that influence your thoughts and response to hunger and appetite. For instance, you may have learnt to ignore your hunger signals when it's not yet mealtime. You may have been told that you shouldn't snack before meals, yet have found yourself at times so hungry by mealtime that you overeat or consume foods that you wouldn't normally.

Foregoing food when you're hungry is likely just one way you've been taught to ignore your hunger. You may have also been taught the behaviour of eating in the absence of hunger, following rules, such as, *it's unhealthy to skip breakfast, eat everything on your plate,* or *if you eat a healthy meal you can then eat dessert.*

Eating to the rules imposed by parents, prescribed meal plans, popular diets or as recommended by health professionals, can all dampen your hunger signals or at least your ability to decipher them. For example, the encouragement by parents to eat more at mealtimes through reasoning, praise and food rewards all contribute to reinforcing the behaviour of eating beyond hunger (72). When a child is told to 'eat just two more bites' or 'try to finish your soup', although intended to encourage children to eat more vegetables, it can inadvertently erode trust in their internal cues and decrease their ability to eat intuitively in response to their hunger and satiety signals. Conversely, restricting a child's access to perceived unhealthy foods can promote future situations of eating these foods in the absence of hunger (73).

If you've unsuccessfully controlled your hunger in the past, sensations of hunger may trigger stress or anxiety for you, rather than simply be a cue to eat. On the other hand, if you pride yourself on your ability to restrict food, you might experience hunger as a good feeling, because you feel powerful or successful when you deny yourself. In this respect, hunger confirms that you are in control.

Alternatively, hunger may trigger fears of going without, causing you to respond to the slightest sensation of hunger. Or you may perceive the physical sensations of hunger as a character weakness or personal failing, as you might believe it represents your inability to control yourself around food. It may be that you only feel satisfied if you're excessively full or that feeling full stimulates feelings of panic, irritability and remorse instead of satisfaction and contentment. Let's look at common hunger signals and use a hunger scale to help you tune into your body and ease these fears.

✍ Are you eating because you are hungry?

Get acquainted with your internal hunger signals

Become familiar with the signals your body exhibits when you feel hungry, such as:

- growling or grumbling in your stomach
- empty or hollow feeling in your stomach
- gnawing feeling in your stomach
- desperation to eat
- feeling queasy
- weakness or low energy
- difficulty concentrating
- dizziness or light-headedness
- slight headache
- irritability or crankiness

Record in your Workbook or journal the signs that most frequently signal to you that you are hungry. Consider how intense these signals become before you eat or whether you ride them until you no longer feel hunger. Observe whether the signs of hunger change as the intensity of your hunger increases. Alternatively, you may rarely feel hunger as you have been following a prescribed meal plan for so long.

Reflect on whether hunger is something you rarely or frequently experience, and whether it is a sensation that you perhaps ignore or fear. Record your thoughts without censoring or judging them. Consider when and where your perceptions and associations with hunger may have originated.

cont.

It is possible that health conditions and medications can alter your hunger signals: they may cause you not to feel hunger or to feel hungry constantly. Talk to your doctor as to how your health condition or medications might interfere with your body's hunger signals. If you constantly feel hungry or have intense hunger signals, it's possible that you're experiencing low blood sugar. If you experience signals such as: irritability, dizziness, light-headedness, confusion, headaches, sleepiness, blurred vision, sweating or irregular heartbeat, consult your doctor. Once you better understand how possible health conditions or medications influence your hunger signals, you'll be in a better position to acknowledge what hunger feels like to you. You'll also know how you need to approach eating to ensure your body is sufficiently nourished.

Hunger Scale

A Hunger Scale is how you'd score your hunger between 1 to 10, with 1 being famished through to 10, where you are stuffed to the point of feeling nauseated.

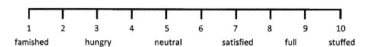

Make a note in your Workbook or journal of what the different levels of hunger feel like to you. You may want to refer back to your previously recorded sensations of hunger for this, or consider the below descriptions.

1. Extremely hungry, lightheaded, headache, no energy.
2. Overly hungry, irritable, stomach growling, constant thoughts of food.
3. Hungry, empty stomach feeling; thinking about food. *This is the ideal hunger level to eat a meal.*

cont.

4. Slightly hungry. *A snack would do, or it's time to start making plans to eat soon.*

5. Neutral, you don't feel hungry or full.

6. Slightly full, you're not quite satisfied and could eat a little more.

7. Comfortably satisfied, you feel you've eaten enough. *This is the optimal time to stop eating.*

8. Slightly too full. It can happen when you unconsciously ate everything on your plate, or were distracted. No problem, wait until you're hungry again to eat. Your next meal may be later or smaller than normal, depending on your hunger level. Next time you eat in similar situations or with similar foods, try to eat consciously.

9. Overly full, uncomfortable, with a feeling you need to bring out the elasticated pants. Later, you may want to investigate why you ate so much. Begin to identify your internal and external triggers, and explore other coping mechanisms.

10. Extremely full, to the point of feeling nauseous or painful. This point of being *stuffed* is likely to be associated with a binge or emotional eating episode, which can cause physical and emotional distress. You cannot change what has already occurred; resisting *what is* creates more pain. Instead, allow these physical sensations to pass. At a later time when you feel neutral hunger, explore what triggered the excessive eating: was it restriction and deprivation, immense hunger, an emotional trigger, an association, habit, self-punishment or to numb out? If these eating episodes occur more than twice a week over a period of weeks or months, seek the support of your doctor or the services of a psychologist or suitably experienced counsellor.

Right now, tune into your body and use the Hunger Scale to determine how hungry or full you are. Try this throughout the day and record your hunger and fullness level before and after eating. Continue this for one week, either by recording your body's signals of hunger or by using the Hunger Scale.

Avoid a Hunger-Fullness Diet

The purpose of using the Hunger Scale is to discern your hunger signals, which indicate when to eat and when to stop eating. As a conscious eater, the intention is to maintain a hunger level between 3 and 7, so that you begin eating when you reach a hunger level of 3-4 and stop eating when your hunger level reaches a fullness of 6-7.

Ideally, you want to avoid either end of the scale: waiting until you're ravenously hungry (2 and below) or eating to the point of your fullness being physically uncomfortable (8 and above). The intention is to maintain a hunger level that minimises subsequent overeating or reduces long periods of restriction to compensate for previous overeating.

You may notice that if you allow yourself to get to a 1 or 2 on the Hunger Scale, you're more likely to then eat to an 8 or above. If you allow yourself to get extremely hungry, it's much harder to eat consciously and choose foods that will feel good to your body. You're more likely to choose to eat anything available, even if you're aware that your body doesn't respond well to it: anything would be better than that gnawing feeling in your stomach.

To aid this new awareness, it can be useful to pause in the middle of a meal or snack and ask yourself: *What is my fullness level? Am I still hungry? Do I wish to continue eating?* This is not to reduce your serving sizes or to stop eating prematurely, but to ensure you are eating for hunger and are sufficiently satisfied.

If you've had an unhealthy relationship with hunger, it can be all too easy to enforce new eating rules by way of a hunger-fullness diet: *eat when hungry and stop eating when full.* Indeed, some media personalities and weight loss programs apply the Hunger Scale with the purpose of weight loss and controlling your intake. However, the more appropriate intention of hunger awareness is not to control your eating, which would do more to perpetuate guilt should you eat when not hungry or eat beyond comfortable fullness, but to become better acquainted with your internal hunger cues. Another reason for using the Hunger Scale is to learn to trust that your body knows *when* and *how much* it requires to sustain you. The intention is to observe your hunger with curiosity and non-judgement, so that you can begin to explore your reasons for why, what, when and how you eat.

Despite the intention of the Hunger Scale, it's perfectly normal on occasion to eat when you're not hungry or to eat a meal and feel that you ate too much, such as when you are dining out or eating your favourite foods. These experiences can provide opportunities to uncover more about your relationship with food and identify triggers that lead to under- or overeating. They don't mean you require greater control over your eating.

Satisfy Your Hunger

I recall an art exhibition where I saw a photograph of a polar bear strolling contently across a barren icy landscape after having devoured a seal. The caption on the photograph stated that the polar bear was in *blissful satiation*.

Satiation, or a feeling of fullness after eating, can bring a feeling of satisfaction and contentment, especially if you were previously ravenously hungry, as this polar bear most probably was. Unfortunately, you can confuse this feeling of satisfaction and contentment with a need to overeat. So rather than simply curbing hunger or feeling satisfied, there is a desire to feel stuffed. I can relate. Years ago, I only felt sufficiently satisfied if I fell into a *food coma* from overindulging.

Even now, my husband still wants the largest slice of pizza or the biggest serve of ice cream. When he eats something that he perceives as indulgent, he is resistant to sharing. For him, the desire to *have it all* and to feel full we believe stems from years of strenuous exercise and consequential ravenous hunger. This immense hunger perpetuated a perception that *if I'm not stuffed, then I am not satisfied.* He also recalls how in his late teens he would prepare or purchase a snack and ask his mother if she wanted any, as he would get more if she did. Her response was frequently 'no', but then she would later dip her hand into his bowl of chips or snap off a line of chocolate. He didn't enjoy not getting to eat all that he had intended to eat, which further exacerbated his desire to *eat it all*.

You may be able to relate to my husband's desire to *eat it all* or eating to the point of feeling stuffed. Eating beyond fullness is a common outcome of dieting, which can create the same ravenous hunger as running a marathon.

Overeating may occur due to immense hunger, in anticipation of future restriction or due to sheer enjoyment of the food you're eating. Eating beyond fullness is normal occasionally. However, an inability to stop eating when you're full is generally fuelled by beliefs about food and yourself, rather than a true physical desire and enjoyment of food. Overeating may be the consequence of thoughts such as: *it's good value for money, so eat as much as you can*—think buffets and supersize options; *I can't eat this normally so I may as well get as much as I can;* or, *make the most of this, as you won't be getting this again till you lose this 10 kg.*

Thoughts like these are the result of your beliefs about food and yourself, and not your hunger and response to food in this moment. To get out of your head—which may tell you how you should or should not eat—draw your attention to the sensations in your body in order to gauge how much to eat. If a food doesn't feel good to your body or you feel overly full, you don't have to eat it all. It won't save starving children in Africa. Conversely, if you eat everything you've served yourself and you don't feel satiated, then consume more or another food till you do. With time, you'll be better able to gauge and prepare sufficient quantities or minimise food wastage. However, this shouldn't be your priority right now.

I now recognise how my hunger levels and response to food changes with time of day, month, mood, physical activity, and so on. For example, rather than feeling guilty for my appetite for additional carbohydrates before menstruation, I acknowledge and honour it. I consume additional bread or potato, or enjoy pizza and pasta when dining out. Through honouring my hunger and requirement for additional energy, I've found that I don't have the same ups and downs of mood and excessive nighttime consumption of chocolate like I used to. Don't get me wrong, I still eat some chocolate at this time. However, unlike previously when I deprived myself, the cravings, and swings in hunger and moods are now less pronounced to non-existent.

Overcoming Your Fear of Hunger

Hunger is not something to be feared. It's not your enemy, intent on sabotaging your weight and health. Hunger is completely innocent and instinctive. It is dieting and external eating rules that erode trust in your hunger signals or your response to them.

Fear of hunger will remain as long as you believe that you can control the sensations of hunger through what and how you eat. Unfortunately, your attempts to control your hunger can lead you to either extreme on the Hunger Scale, neither of which promote balance and trust in your hunger signals.

Welcome, allow and feel hunger

If you fear being hungry and compulsively eat as soon as any sensations of hunger strike, you may find it useful to recall a time when you thought you were *starving* and then got distracted. Perhaps you were enjoying yourself so much that you forgot to eat, and you no longer noticed hunger. Recalling these times may help you to see that the hunger you felt didn't require immediate attention. You may well have needed to eat, but you were not at risk of passing away as a consequence. Acknowledging this may enable you to be more relaxed when hunger strikes, and eat more calmly and consciously. However, I'm not suggesting you employ this as a tool to control or *power through* your hunger.

If you do feel a need to eat as soon as hunger strikes, you may find it useful to explore your hunger sensations further, to assess whether you're truly hungry. When you first experience hunger, rather than resist the sensation or eat immediately, allow it to be. Welcome and allow the feeling of hunger. Then *feel* into the sensations of hunger. Explore where you feel the sensations. You may have thought you had a growling stomach, yet when you draw your awareness to it, you realise that the sensation was in your chest. You may discover that it's not hunger that you're feeling but, for example, tension or nervousness. Alternatively, you may find that the hunger either dissipates or intensifies when you focus on it. Notice the sensations of hunger, delaying eating for a few moments to determine if you're physically hungry or not.

The intention of welcoming and allowing your hunger is not to control or ignore it, but to ensure that you're truly feeling hungry. And that you're interpreting the signals correctly and responding to them appropriately.

Conversely, you may be a pro at *riding your hunger*, having trained yourself to dissipate your hunger so that the sensations disappear and you can avoid eating a snack or meal. You may have mastered this so that hunger and eating don't distract you from your work, or as a weight management tool. As a consequence, you may have *forgotten* the feeling of hunger. If this is the case for you, you may find that establishing an eating routine is beneficial to reacquaint yourself with hunger.

When you begin to eat, do so tuning into your hunger signals every so often to gauge whether you've eaten enough and when it's time to stop eating. You don't have to chew your food forty times or follow similar prescriptions to slow your intake. The intention is not to eat less, but to eat with your full awareness of each mouthful and how it feels to your body.

There is no perfect speed at which to eat. Though it can be helpful to remember that it takes between ten and thirty minutes for your stomach and brain to register feelings of fullness (74). Therefore, gobbling down your meal can cause you to eat beyond a fullness level of 8, and can also reduce the sensory satisfaction of food consumption.

A fear of hunger can cause you to eat insufficient or excessive quantities of food as well as generate distrust of yourself around food. You may have placed more trust in the rules and beliefs of others than your own body, such as *breakfast is the most important meal of the day,* or, *you shouldn't eat after 8 pm.* By placing greater faith in *the rules* than your hunger, you may ignore your hunger at 8 pm, to then find yourself taking a midnight snack or overeating the following morning. This unplanned or excessive eating can perpetuate feelings of guilt and shame, and thus does more to erode trust in your body than to support a healthy relationship with food.

Fear of judgement by others can also impact your response to hunger. You may fear what others think of you relative to what you're eating and so override your hunger signals. For example, although you may be extremely hungry, you don't want to be seen eating, or if you do eat, you may choose something insufficient for fear of appearing *piggish*. The immense hunger that may ensue can lead to excessive eating behind closed doors by way of *secret eating*.

Whether others judge you for your eating or not has nothing to do with you. You cannot control others' thoughts of you. It is their own beliefs that lead them to see the world as they do. Even if they stare or make comments, it can only hurt or shame you if you believe it to be true. You can rebut their remarks to alert them to comments that can be hurtful. However, you can do so in a calmer and more open-minded way when you have released attempting to control their thinking.

Honour your hunger

The best judge of how much or what you should eat is your own body. Tune into your hunger and honour your internal cues of hunger and satiety, rather than allow others' perception of you dictate your actions. To honour your hunger:

1. Take the time to tune into your body when hunger strikes.
2. Welcome, allow, and feel hunger without instantly or automatically quietening it with food.
3. Determine if it's true hunger you're feeling, or another non-physical need or desire.
4. Remove yourself from distractions before you eat, and eat with your full awareness.
5. Tune into your level of hunger as you eat.
6. Discontinue eating when you're sufficiently satisfied that the food you've eaten will sustain you for three to four hours.

Your Hunger and Fullness Responses
to Specific Foods

The physical sensations of hunger and its intensity not only depend on *when* you last ate but also *what* you ate. It has been theorised, and many diet proponents claim, that the macronutrient composition of a meal—the proportion of protein, fat and carbohydrates—affects satiation and appetite, and consequently, the interval between meals and the intensity of hunger experienced (75,76).

Further, satiation and proceeding hunger is not only influenced by macronutrient composition but also by the viscosity and enjoyment of the food. For example, studies have reported that fluid calories, such as beverages, are less satiating than their solid equivalents (77,78,79). This explains why diet shakes that are nutritionally adequate rarely provide the same satisfaction as a small meal of equivalent calories; they certainly never satisfied my hunger.

As well as the influence of macronutrient composition and food substance, research indicates that hunger signals may be less intense when consuming a diet comprised predominantly of *wholefoods* as compared to highly-processed and refined foods. A study that compared the perceived hunger signals of people on a calorie-dense and nutrient-poor, standard American diet, to those on a diet of nutrient-dense wholefoods, found that the frequency and intensity of hunger decreased when people switched to nutrient dense foods (82). As a consequence of the more intense sensations of hunger on the poor nutritional regimen, participants tended to eat even before the previous meal was thoroughly digested, leading to overeating. Further, mood fluctuations associated with hunger were more extreme, with participants experiencing greater irritability with hunger on the poor nutritional diet.

With this in mind, take notice of the effect of different foods on your sensations of hunger, and consider how soon you become hungry after consuming them. For example, I feel the hunger after a sugary snack far more intensely than after other foods. Sugary snacks cause me to feel jittery or light-headed. The subsequent hunger feels more frantic, so that obtaining my next sustenance feels much more desperate than normal. Knowing my response to sugary foods, at times I now choose to eat more fat, protein or fibre with sugary treats. At other times, I may choose a low sugar option or simply ensure that my next meal is nutritionally balanced.

If I feel that I may become anxious about an important task or being somewhere on time, I may forgo a sugary treat as I know it will likely exacerbate the jittery feeling. However, if my intended day is restful, I may choose to eat the sugary snack. The decision is based on how I feel and want to feel on any particular day, rather than rules I have imposed on myself.

Joyful Eating Principle 4.
OBSERVE AND SATISFY YOUR HUNGER

A fear or distrust of your hunger signals is frequently the
result of dieting and imposing external rules on yourself. Get
acquainted with your internal hunger cues and learn to trust that
your body knows when to eat and how much food it requires
to sustain you. More often than not, eat when you're physically
hungry, and stop eating when you're sufficiently satiated.

12

Abandon Labelling Food as Good or Bad

"Sometimes surrender means giving up trying to understand and becoming comfortable with not knowing."

— Eckhart Tolle

Children interact with the world with utter curiosity. At a young age, this curiosity is uninhibited by beliefs of what is good or bad, right or wrong, or how they should or should not behave. A baby becomes aware of their body through observing their fingers in motion or grabbing at their feet. A toddler explores their awareness of self through touching and holding objects; often shaking, biting and chewing to discover what the properties of the object are.

If you were to maintain the curiosity of a baby or toddler your entire life, without labelling objects and foods, you wouldn't get very far. Mentally labelling objects, experiences and people assigns them into categories in your mind, ensuring your safety and intellectual development so that you can act appropriately the next time you encounter similar circumstances. It has served humans, in an evolutionary sense, by preventing people from eating poisonous berries, rotten meat and from scalding ourselves. If every time you went to drink coffee you were unaware that coffee might be hot, you would not drink with caution or test the temperature before drinking. Having an understanding that coffee may be hot, or that moving cars are dangerous, or that dogs can react in unexpected ways, enables you to anticipate certain scenarios before they occur. This increases the likelihood of your survival and appropriate behaviour. The labelling and categorising of objects and experiences is primal; even a gazelle needs to place all cats into the category of *dangerous* to stay alive.

Not only is it your innate nature to label objects, people or experiences, but you are taught certain labels throughout your childhood. Parents, in their role to protect their children from danger, but also to increase their children's ability to interact and behave in a socially acceptable way, teach their children to distinguish right from wrong. They teach their children not to touch certain objects, not to place unknown objects in their mouth, or to make noise through banging objects together. Siblings, peers and teachers may reinforce these *labels,* so that over time you develop a perception of the most appropriate way to behave to gain the love and acceptance of those you love and respect. You are taught that certain behaviours, people, food or objects are good or bad, yummy or yucky, pretty or ugly, fat or skinny, smart or stupid and so on. Therefore, you not only form labels and categories to explain and comprehend the world around you, but you also adopt those of other people and the society in which you live.

Despite the crucial role that labelling plays in your safety and social interactions, the downfall is that once you reach adulthood, you may have lost your sense of curiosity. As an adult, you can be quick to label and categorise without fully engaging your senses and being present with *what is.* Consequently, you can erroneously label or categorise objects, experiences and people based on past events, without exploring whether these labels hold true in the experience occurring right now.

More specifically, you may perceive you like or dislike a food based on past experiences, without engaging your senses in the moment. You may mindlessly eat because you know, for example, what a pear tastes like, and can eat it while distracted. Although you don't require your full awareness

151

every time you take a sip of coffee to prevent yourself from scalding your mouth, eating and drinking can provide you with the opportunity to tune into your body, quieten your mind and incite the relaxation response.

Labelling Food

The pursuit of the perfect diet has resulted in more confusion and stress about what and how to eat than at any previous time. For much of the '80s and '90s, many diets focused on reducing fat, because per gram, fat provides twice as much energy to the body as protein and carbohydrates. Although logical, the production of no-fat, low-fat or diet products led people to eat these foods with abandon due to the perception that all these products were healthy.

Consequently, health on a population level didn't improve, and in fact, other health complications ensued. The intake of fats that are essential for the cell membranes, hormones and other vital functions became insufficient in some chronic dieters. A further complication was that to make the low-fat food taste better, food technologists added more refined sugars and artificial flavours to these foods, thus increasing total sugar, and in some instances, caloric intake.

In rebellion to the low-fat craze, there has been a recent rise in *health gurus* who apply the logic that if fat wasn't as bad as previously thought, it must be good. This thinking has initiated a wave of high-fat, low-sugar or low-carbohydrate diets. Some of these diets are excessively high in fat plus deficient in other nutrients required for good health. Therefore, the scales have been tipped too far in the opposite direction.

Unfortunately, this black and white thinking, otherwise known as binary thinking, creates an either-or mentality, where foods are considered as either *good* or *bad*. Binary thinking can lead to an all-or-nothing rationale: if excessive consumption of a certain food is bad and reducing its intake is good, then eliminating it entirely from your diet must be *best*. Or the opposite: if a food is good, then eating more of it must be better... *you can never have too much of a good thing.* However, neither extreme, inadequacy nor excess, are healthy.

The issue with binary thinking is that no food is good or bad in absolute terms, as it depends on the frequency and quantity of your intake, and your unique body and lifestyle. Let's explore this, taking sugar as an example.

Most government dietary guidelines state that excessive sugar consumption is undesirable for your health. Yet this doesn't make sugar unequivocally bad. Where do you *draw a line* in the sugar grains to declare that this much sugar is good and that much sugar is bad?

The *line* is arbitrary. It is established on probability, not absolute truth. There are so many factors to consider in your overall health and well-being. Eating a particular food or adopting a certain lifestyle habit provides no guarantee of good health for you.

If you rely on guidelines and recommendations instead of your body to guide what you eat, you can easily sabotage yourself. So that, if you consume sugar, chocolate or wine, you can justify your consumption, thinking: *a little won't hurt,* or *chocolate and wine are good for you.* It is possible to find contradictory scientific evidence in support of a food being either healthy or unhealthy. So that if you were inclined to justify or refute consuming chocolate, coffee, wine, meat, bread or potatoes, you could probably find evidence that they are either healthy or unhealthy.

Furthermore, experience and observation have shown you that a teaspoon of sugar won't kill you and that there are both health benefits and concerns with eating chocolate and drinking wine. So, you can choose to believe whatever suits you in the moment. Plus, when you resist the temptation of sugar, chocolate or wine, you might feel righteous for foregoing them. On the other hand, when you give in to temptation, you might feel weak and pathetic.

If you eat what you perceive as bad food, you may think, *I have ruined today, so I may as well continue eating crap food. Hey, If I can't be good, I may as well be bad.* In this respect, your perception of food as good or bad can perpetuate feeling good or bad about yourself: you've attached your sense of self-worth to your eating.

Other times, you may desire food because you feel that you deserve a *treat*. You may feel you've earned a reward or compensation for your hard work, commitment to a task, or an achievement. When eating originates from the perception that you deserve to eat poorly because you've been good, you may find yourself eating foods because you perceive them as treats, rather than based on enjoyment and sensations in your body.

Alternatively, you may consume *treat foods* in anticipation of the hard work ahead. You may eat treat foods before you undertake a difficult or daunting task, as you fear that if you don't achieve it, you will miss out. You may think, *the chocolate bar is there for me anyway, whether I succeed or not*. If you consume the chocolate bar before you've finished the task, it can perpetuate guilt and shame. It may reinforce the belief that you can't, or won't, achieve what you set out to do. You may end up eating the chocolate whenever you feel like you're unable to achieve, or feel you have failed at the task. However, when you no longer view food as either good or bad, you may find that your thoughts and desires about those foods you considered as bad dissipate.

Consider this: what if sugar, chocolate, wine and doughnuts were neither good nor bad? What if you instead focused on your enjoyment of them and investigated how they feel to your body? Thus, allowing your physical, mental and emotional responses to food to be the barometer as to what to eat and how much.

How would your relationship with food change if you focused on the sensory experience of eating, rather than whether you're eating right or wrong? What if you could decide whether to eat a doughnut based on how it makes you feel and the joy it brings you, rather than focusing on the labels and beliefs that often originate from external sources?

✍ Good or bad foods

On two separate pages in your Workbook or journal, list foods that you consider as:

1. good or healthy, and
2. bad or unhealthy.

Then, beside each food item, record the reason or information that reinforces this belief.

Consider how the lists of what you categorise as good or bad foods can change, often based on the latest popular diet being promoted in the media. Is there anything in your good list that you or society would have considered as bad in the past, or vice versa?

How do you think your food choices would be influenced if there were no good or bad food list in your mind? If a food wasn't labelled as bad, do you think there would be the same desire to eat it? If you consider that you don't gain more energy from 150 calories of fruit and yogurt than 150 calories of pizza, does this change how you would categorise foods?

Can you see how the concept of food being good or bad in absolute terms is flawed?

You may feel resistance to this, as although the calories of a pizza may be the same as fruit and yogurt, the nutritional quality is not equal. That may be true. However, that does not make pizza bad, and fruit and yogurt good.

Based on these considerations, is there any food that you would now move from one list to the other? Are there any foods you feel would be more appropriate in a *neutral* list? Go through the two lists and place an asterisk (*) beside any foods that you would now consider as neutral.

How Encouraging Healthy Eating Can Backfire

For some people, labelling food as *healthy* can actually create negative connotations and resistance to these foods.

Contrary to the intention of many parents attempting to encourage their children to eat sufficient quantities of healthy food, they can inadvertently create an aversion to these foods. Pressuring children to eat foods that are considered good for them has been shown to lower fruit and vegetable intake and increase picky eating (83), and this aversion to healthy foods can persist throughout life (84). As an adult, you may avoid certain foods as you experience the food through your perception that *healthy food is boring, tasteless, ordinary, plain, disgusting* or *yuk*, rather than your five senses.

I've met people that resist any food that is allegedly good for them. In some instances, I've not divulged the healthy or unusual ingredients, such as beetroot or zucchini in a cake, or lentils in rissoles, until the food has been devoured. Only then, when I disclose the healthy ingredients, do some people display pleasant surprise… while others revulsion. It's not the sensory experience of the food, but the thoughts and beliefs about the food, that creates this response. Scientific experiments have confirmed that people perceive food to be tastier if they believe it to be unhealthy (85).

Not only do the labels ascribed to food reinforce an aversion to healthy food, restricting foods perceived as unhealthy can increase a child's desire to obtain and consume these foods, even in the absence of hunger (73,86). Thus, restricting food can foster an increased liking, intake and overeating of these so-called unhealthy foods.

How the 'Health Halo' Effect Can Lead to Overeating

Not only does labelling foods as *healthy* potentially lead to an aversion to these foods and an increased liking of unhealthy foods, the perception that a food is healthy can also lead to greater consumption of that food, or justification of additional eating because of good eating behaviour

(87,88,89). You've probably done this yourself; eaten a healthy meal, and then justified eating dessert. This perception is known as the *health halo effect*, where a food is categorised as intrinsically good or bad, healthy or unhealthy, regardless of how much is eaten (90,91,88,92).

In a survey of over 180 college students in the United States, almost half believed that typical high-calorie foods in small amounts contain more calories than typical low-calorie foods in much larger amounts, and classified foods according to a good versus bad dichotomy (90). This binary thinking resulted in the belief that they could eat more of a healthy food or could eat more unhealthy foods after choosing a healthy food, without feeling guilty or gaining weight (90,91,92).

Food companies are aware of the importance of labelling foods as healthy, including embedding health terms in the product title itself, such as *low-fat chocolate chip muffins, all-natural muesli slice,* or *high protein bar.* Health labelling can increase consumption of these foods, and often discourages people from seeking further nutritional information about the product (96,97). Unfortunately, these terms may not mean that the product is *healthier* or has lower calories than comparable products. However, your perception that it *is* might increase your likelihood of purchasing and thus consuming it.

I'm not saying there is any conspiracy or that food companies are malicious. Food companies need to make a profit, just like you and I. All marketing, whether of food, entertainment, fashion or homewares, is intended to encourage you to purchase and consume products. Food companies can appear deceptive and immoral, as they feed right into the binary thinking of food as good or bad, healthy or unhealthy. However, rather than thinking food labelling should be different and feeling angry or resentful, you could choose to ignore food labelling and not allow it to sway your purchases. Until you release your preoccupation with weight loss and health, food companies will continue to play to your fears and desires.

Your Morality is Not Bound to Your Eating

The experiences and knowledge you acquire about food throughout your life not only generates a partitioning of food as good or bad but can establish a perception that your morality and self-worth is connected to your eating. A child may be told, 'you're such a good boy for eating all your spinach', or you may hear a parent say, 'I can't believe I ate all that cake, I am so naughty/bad/disgusting/ashamed'. The messages you receive from your parents, peers, teachers, society, media and medical professionals can reinforce a belief that if you eat well, you are good, and if you eat unhealthily or excessively, you are bad. However, food is neither good nor bad; it is just food. If you eat food that you or society perceives as bad, it does not make you bad. The saying, *you are what you eat* is not literal. Food has no morality except for what you ascribe to it.

To interrupt this thinking, it is necessary to discontinue labelling food as good or bad, and instead experience it for the sensory input it provides and the feelings it creates in your body. This involves engaging all your senses when you eat, rather than eating in response to the thoughts in your mind. Thoughts that tell you what you *should* or *should not* eat, thoughts that continually assess your food choices and eating behaviour. Once food is no longer good or bad, you can no longer attach your morality to it.

When food is neither good nor bad, you can experience it for what it truly is. You can really taste a piece of fruit and sense its juiciness, without thinking, *this is good for me*, or *I am good*. Conversely, you can consume a doughnut and enjoy the sensory experience without the incessant thoughts: *I shouldn't be eating this, this is so bad for me*, or *I have blown my diet*.

You may feel resistance to ditching your food labels, as you believe you would simply eat everything and anything with complete abandon. But this response is likely the result of *diet mentality*, not a desire or liking of the food. Once you are secure in knowing that you can have any food whenever you want without restriction, the desire for it is likely to dissipate, while the desire for other foods seen as healthy may increase. When you ditch the food labels and associated rules, you'll be better able to learn to eat in a way that satisfies, nourishes and feels good to your body and mind.

13

Ditch Your Diet and Food Rules

"There is no list of rules. There is one rule. The rule is: there are no rules. Happiness comes from living as you need to, as you want to. As your inner voice tells you to. Happiness comes from being who you actually are instead of who you think you are supposed to be."

—Shonda Rhimes, *Year of Yes*

I recall a time I went to dinner with a friend who had been learning to embrace mindful eating. We went to a restaurant that has a mouth-watering display of cakes and chocolates. We looked over the menu. Although it was full of delicious and nourishing meals, nothing inspired us at that moment.

After scouring the menu, my friend said, 'I think I'm going to start with dessert because they're so good here. And to be honest, that's the main reason I come to this restaurant.' I wholeheartedly agreed. So, we both decided to start with dessert.

After eating the sensationally rich and creamy chocolate cake, I still felt a little hungry, but now wanted something light and fresh. So, I ordered a salad. If I'd eaten the meal the other way around, I'd probably have started with a heavier meal, choosing the pizza or quinoa burger that I'd eaten there before. These meals would have more than satisfied me, yet I would still have eaten the cake, as that too is the real reason I venture to this restaurant. As a result, I would have eaten beyond satisfied.

Eating dessert after a main meal is just one of the many eating rules common in our society. Eating rules originate from society, your family, friends, past experiences and diets. Eating rules are learnt at the dinner table, in the schoolyard, through books, magazines and social media. Diets, whether for weight loss or health, are essentially a set of rules to follow to attain desired outcomes. Supposedly, you can measure your success not only by the results you attain but by how well you've followed the rules.

Rules can provide a sense of control. If you believe you cannot trust yourself or your body, it makes sense that you'd feel *safer* around food, and more in control, when you have rules to keep yourself *in line*. However, it's more likely that it's your attempts to abide by the rules that causes your eating to spiral *out of control*—not that you cannot trust yourself or your body.

Following food rules can perpetuate an all-or-nothing mindset or even awaken your inner rebel. Your inner rebel is the part of you that desires to *break* or defy the rules. It's the part of you that says, *you can't tell me what to do!* Your inner rebel may chime in when you're tired of being *good* or you feel you've earned some time without the restraint of rules.

Unfortunately, or fortunately, depending on your perspective, food can be a socially acceptable means to defy the rules in life. However, whether the rules are your own or originate from an external source, the person you often end up hurting is yourself.

✎ Identify your eating and food rules

Throughout the next week, in your Workbook or journal, record any eating rules that come to mind or those that you have thought in the past regarding what, when, why and how you *should* or *should not* eat. These could include rules about:

- types of food
- quality of food
- calories
- portion sizes
- preparation of food
- time of eating
- what constitutes a meal
- snacks
- drinks

If you find it hard to identify your food rules, notice when you say to yourself or others the words *should* or *must*. For example, *I should have something to eat now; I really shouldn't eat all this potato; I shouldn't have eaten that ice cream; I must refrain from eating the remainder of the cake.* The words *should* or *must* provide a good indication that there is an underlying rule.

Once you've recorded your eating and food rules in your Workbook or journal, consider the following:

- How did I come up with this rule?
- Is it based on facts or fears?
- What happens if I break this rule?
- What would happen if I could eat what I want when I want?
- What foods or behaviours am I afraid of if I were to let go of my food rules?
- Would I be comfortable telling anyone else about this rule or to follow this rule—why or why not?

cont.

- What am I giving up by following this rule?
- What do I gain by following this rule?
- How has this rule served me in the past?
- Does it serve me to hold on to this rule?
- Do I plan on following this rule forever?

Through this reflection begin to challenge your rules and explore how you feel about the idea of letting them go.

Eating and Food Rules

Let's explore some commonly held diet, eating and food rules. Through these examples, you'll hopefully begin to see how rules take you out of the moment and disconnect you from your body.

Diet Rule: Eating to the clock

Have you ever found yourself finishing off a substantial brunch or morning tea, to then think about what to have for lunch... not because you're hungry but because it soon will be lunchtime? Alternatively, have you come home ravenous and snacked on chips, crackers, nuts or cheese to ward off your hunger until dinnertime... because you didn't believe you should eat dinner yet?

Eating to a schedule can cause undereating or overeating, depending on the eating timetable and food quantities you have devised for yourself or those imposed by a diet program. Consequently, you might automatically eat just because it's time to eat. Or else you may *push through your hunger,* causing yourself to overeat, eat quickly or mindlessly when you finally do allow yourself to eat. Either way, it can perpetuate a disconnect to your body's signals of hunger and satiation.

I had a client who was following a strict eating schedule. When I talked with her about eating when she was hungry, she was unaware of what hunger felt like for her. She never allowed herself to get hungry. Letting go of her rule of *eating to the clock* enabled her to awaken and tune into her hunger signals and thus eat based on what her body required, rather than her eating plan. In her case, eating to a schedule was her mechanism to avert a fear of gaining weight. For others, a fear of hunger may drive their eating, as they believe if they eat according to the clock they will never have to feel the ensuing emptiness.

Some people I've worked with would arrive home ravenously hungry after a long day at work, and find themselves snacking on anything they could get their hands on to tide them over till dinner. Once they let go of the rule of eating dinner at a specific time, they could eat a more substantial meal earlier, without guilt. Or they could choose a smaller serve at dinner if they were not all that hungry due to their afternoon snacking.

Letting go of the rule of *when to eat* created a substantial shift in my own relationship with food. It enabled me to eat whenever and whatever suited my body at any given time. Now, I may consume dinner anywhere from four to nine o'clock, depending on how I feel and what I have done during the day. I've dropped the rule of eating simply because it's time to eat, and instead honour my hunger.

I acknowledge that regular eating plays an important role in maintaining your energy, keeping your blood sugar levels stable and your metabolism firing. Just remember, strict dedication to eating by the clock can contribute to you ignoring your hunger signals. I encourage you to investigate for yourself whether your eating is in response to signals from your body, or in time with the clock.

Diet Rule: Three square meals

Since dropping the rule of needing to eat to a schedule, I now eat when I'm hungry and eat till the hunger has subsided. I no longer consume what would be considered *normal* to eat at a specific time of the day: that is, what constitutes breakfast, lunch, dinner and snacks. Sometimes at *meal time,* I eat a substantial meal, yet at other times it is fruit, a snack or solely a dessert.

Eating an afternoon snack won't spoil your dinner. The only thing that can spoil your dinner is eating simply because it's dinner time, without hunger or focus. You don't need to eat dinner if you are not hungry, and you don't need to eat everything on your plate if you are no longer hungry.

There are many guidelines as to what constitutes an adequate meal. However, so long as your diet is nutritionally balanced over the day or week, it's not essential that every meal is nutritionally balanced. Instead, focus on what you feel like eating and what sustains your energy until your next meal without you becoming ravenously hungry. As you begin to base your decision to eat or not eat on your internal cues, you may determine certain foods or proportions of fat, protein and carbohydrates that suit you best, to provide sustained energy.

Diet Rule: Eat everything on your plate

Another common rule that you may have been taught, and continue to this day, is to finish everything on your plate. You may have been told, or believe that:

- the cook (mum) has worked hard to make a good dinner, and I should eat out of respect
- I shouldn't be wasteful and should eat everything on my plate— *think of all the starving children in the world*
- I've paid for it, so I should get the full value out of it
- I shouldn't be rude and inconsiderate—I must take a piece of auntie's fruitcake
- I should fill up now as I don't want to be hungry later
- if I eat all my vegetables, I can have dessert afterwards

If you follow these or similar rules, you are eating quantities predetermined in your mind or by others, rather than tuning in and determining what your body requires. However, the volume of food on your plate, whether served by yourself or someone else, may not be the right amount to satisfy and sustain you. The amount of food on your plate is completely arbitrary and needn't dictate the quantity you eat.

Instead of eating to the volume on your plate, draw your attention to your internal cues of hunger and satiety, and allow them to guide how much you eat. Discontinue eating when you are no longer hungry. Serve yourself more if you're not quite satisfied, or prepare yourself an additional snack.

Diet Rule: Dessert after mains

Sometimes a meal is not considered complete unless followed with dessert. Now, there's nothing wrong with eating dessert, especially if you're hungry or have intentionally *left room*. However, the consumption of dessert can often be the result of external cues, rather than your internal cues of hunger and recognition of how the food makes you feel. Eating dessert to the point of being absolutely *stuffed* can erode trust in yourself around dessert, and lead you to believe your eating is out of control.

Dessert also has associations beyond hunger, enjoyment, or a perception of a complete meal. Throughout your life, you may have learned to consider dessert as entertainment, a distraction, a reward or a bribe. It is common practise to provide a child with dessert after dinner as a reward or bribe: 'you won't get dessert till you finish your greens', or 'there will be no dessert tonight if you don't finish your homework'. Consequently, dessert can become an expectation after a meal if you have behaved well. It's no wonder that as an adult you may feel you deserve a dessert if you've been good, worked hard, had a tough day, feel hurt or sad. This association with desserts can result in the decision to eat dessert based on your morality or emotions, rather than hunger, the pleasure of eating the food or how the food feels in your body.

If you regularly find yourself finishing dinner with dessert, notice this, and then ask yourself: am I eating dessert because:

- I am still slightly hungry and enjoy this?
- The meal was not satisfying (not enough or didn't satisfy my palate)?
- It's a habit to eat dessert, whether I am hungry or not?
- I was tempted by the dessert on offer, despite being sufficiently or overly full?

Once you are aware of why you're eating dessert, you can then determine whether you need to tune into your hunger or eat more consciously, whether you need to address the meals you prepare, or whether it is a behaviour you need to explore—either to break the habit or investigate your beliefs and associations with dessert.

Diet Rule: Only eat 'junk food' on the weekend or a 'cheat day'

Some diets allow *cheat days*, where you can consume foods that are *out of bounds* on the diet. Cheat days enable you to reward or spoil yourself for your diligence on a diet.

In my twenties, I'd eat like a sparrow during the week, to then devour foods that were out of bounds on the weekend. I'd often feel the need to finish off a batch of brownies or leftover cheesecake so that I could start the diet or controlled eating on Monday. In this way, the allowance of cheat days can backfire, as it can lead to eating for no other reason than you will soon not be allowed to eat these foods, as is the case with the last supper effect. In this way, cheat days can erode trust in yourself around certain foods due to bouts of uncontrollable eating or overeating.

The thing is, cheat days don't in any way promote being mindful when eating, *listening* to your body or even eating foods that make you feel good. Instead, eating is fuelled by the desire to *break* the rules and to eat foods simply because you are (or soon will be) deprived of them. Any eating plan that allows for cheat days remains a diet.

Diet Rule: Eat less, exercise more

Health professionals and the wider public believe that if overweight people ate less and exercised more, they wouldn't be overweight. I naively believed this for much of my twenties. Although I was not overweight, I believed that if I kept reducing my food intake and increasing the intensity and duration of my exercise, I'd achieve the weight and body I desired. Similarly, it's common to hear someone say as they take a second serve, or eat something considered indulgent, 'I'll have to burn this off later'.

The perception that more exercise will expend the energy you consume can prompt over-exercising, or anxiety if you can't exercise or believe you haven't exercised frequently or intensely enough. Years ago, if I couldn't exercise for any reason, I'd feel angst due to my belief that I had to exercise to a high intensity every day.

Regular exercise is a healthy behaviour; however, if it becomes obsessive or a cause of anxiety and stress, you may want to explore your beliefs around exercise. Let's say you perceive that only a one-hour exercise session is sufficient; this belief can prevent you from doing *any* exercise if you're short on time. However, any amount of movement can be beneficial to your body, even if it's substantially less than what you normally do or aspire to do.

Sometimes the best thing you can do for your body is take time to rest. Pushing yourself when you're tired or unwell is likely to have more negative than positive consequences, especially as over-exercising can increase stress hormones and slow your metabolism. Therefore, rather than ascribing to external rules on how frequently and intensely you should exercise, tune into your body to determine when and how it wants to be moved.

Release Your Diet and Food Rules

Hopefully, you're now more aware of your dominant diet and food rules that influence your food choices and eating behaviour. You may believe that your food rules have kept your eating or weight in check (or at least they would if you could stick to them!)

Your diet and food rules have quite possibly served a role in the past, even if to please a parent or to fit in with a group of friends or colleagues. Unfortunately, your food rules can cause you to place greater trust in the rules than in your own body. Once you release your food labels and rules, you'll be better able to discover the foods your body truly desires in order to feel most energetic and alive.

You are likely to become aware of more diet and food rules with time through observing your eating behaviours, along with associated emotions and thoughts. Let's say you notice that your own or someone else's eating behaviour annoys or bothers you; consider what rules are being broken. For instance, if you feel resentment towards another for not cleaning off their plate at a restaurant, or when you finish everything on your plate when it appeared to be too large a serve, notice the thoughts and emotions that arise. Your thoughts provide insight into the rules that have been broken.

Try to go beyond the immediate thought. So, for example, if you're annoyed that you finished everything on your plate when it appeared to be too large a serve for you, you could ask yourself: *Why did I eat everything on my plate when it appeared to be too large a serve? Was it because I was immensely hungry? Was it because it was irresistibly delicious and I enjoyed every mouthful? Was it simply because it was on my plate? Was it that I was eating distracted, and didn't notice I'd eaten it all till it was gone? Was it that I felt I'd be letting someone down if I didn't eat it?*

Then you may ask yourself: *how much should I have eaten? What should I have done or not done? What would be the consequences if I didn't eat everything on my plate; who would be disappointed or who would I be defying? What does it mean about me that I ate all that food?* Your answers to these questions will help you uncover more of your diet and food rules.

However, do be gentle on yourself as you uncover your diet and food rules. You don't need to dissect your every diet and food rule all-at-once or every time you eat. It is likely an ongoing process, as you'll continually uncover rules that may not have been previously apparent.

If a rule still serves you and you feel resistance to ditching it, it may *not* be time to let it go. Begin with letting go of the rules that cause you stress, anxiety, under- or overeating, guilt, shame, blame or emotional disturbance.

Furthermore, take caution not to form a new rule that you must eat consciously or in response to your hunger and satiety cues everytime you eat. When you remember, you do, and when you don't, you don't.

Joyful Eating Principle 5.
DITCH FOOD LABELS AND DIET RULES

Labelling food as either good or bad, healthy or unhealthy, perpetuates perceived *cravings*, temptation for *forbidden* foods, overeating and eating to rebel against the *food rules*. Your food rules and labels keep you trapped in diet mentality and diet cycling. Liberate yourself by eating intuitively to your body's internal cues.

14

Navigate Your Food and Mood Connection

"The peace that comes with surrendered action turns to a sense of aliveness when you actually enjoy what you are doing."

— Eckhart Tolle

When I was living in Singapore, there was a time that I was riding the bus, and diagonally across from me was a boy of about eight, sitting with his mother. The boy was grumpy and whiny, with tears welling up in his eyes. Although I was unaware of what the problem was, I could see that he was tired and fed up. The mother momentarily attempted to console him with words, but then reached into her bag and presented him with an individual serve of biscuits in a small packet. The boy considered the offering, and with what appeared to be defeat, began to eat the biscuits quietly.

The use of food to comfort, soothe, quieten or bribe a child to behave is commonplace. Food is such a simple and accessible comfort that it can become a similar reflex to putting a pacifier in the mouth of a crying baby. The use of food in this way establishes and reinforces the use of food to comfort, preoccupy, distract, ignore or numb your feelings. It is, therefore, no wonder that as an adult you might continue to use food in this way, where you eat to amplify or suppress your emotions.

An emotional connection to food and eating is completely normal. Eating can play a role in reducing stress and irritability while increasing calmness and improving mood (52). It's completely normal on occasion to use food as a comfort, a reward, or even a form of procrastination or distraction.

The common term *comfort food* generally applies to foods that you associate with fond memories or a sense of safety, security, love. Interestingly, research has demonstrated that when food tastes good or has a positive emotion associated with it at the time of eating, your body may develop an emotional connection to that food through what's known as the mesolimbic reward system (38). The comfort of food is not all in your head!

However, emotional eating can become a concern when:

- it becomes your most predominant form of eating or your primary means to soothe your emotions
- it causes you to repeatedly under-eat or overeat, causing your hunger to swing between either extreme on the Hunger Scale
- you frequently eat to comfort or numb yourself from your emotions, or to inflict pain on yourself as a punishment for thoughts or emotions you are feeling
- you overeat because no amount of food seems sufficient to fill the emotional void

However, even if you occasionally compulsively or emotionally eat, it's not the worst thing you could do. Food is a significantly less harmful substance to cope with emotional distress than some other addictive substances. Fighting and struggling against what you perceive as an undesirable behaviour can inadvertently reinforce and amplify it. And no amount of self-reprimanding and guilt will change what has occurred.

Eating for emotional reasons is not a personal weakness or character flaw. Try to accept your emotional eating without judgement or any intention of controlling it. Then explore it with impartial curiosity to uncover the emotional triggers for eating and alternative ways to deal with your emotions without food, where possible.

Emotional Triggers

The emotional triggers for eating or not eating are very individual and circumstantial. An emotional state may cause one person to eat and yet suppress another person's appetite. Therefore, it's necessary to determine for yourself the emotional triggers that contribute to your decision to eat (or not eat) and the associated eating behaviours.

Keeping a *Food and Mood Journal* can help to increase awareness of your emotional reasons for eating. Awareness of the emotions that trigger certain food choices and eating behaviours can help to identify what you truly require and other ways to cope with your emotions without food.

Yet, this doesn't mean you will no longer eat for emotional reasons. If you feel too emotionally distressed in the moment, don't resist emotional eating; don't force yourself to do things you don't want to. You may need to wait until later, when you're in a more neutral state of mind, to explore strategies that you could adopt to reduce emotional distress in similar situations in the future. The intention is not to cease emotional eating, but to adopt strategies other than eating, more often than not.

When I'm physically and emotionally tired, as I've given so much of my attention and energy to others, I might reflexively reach for food. Rather than guilting myself to stop this eating behaviour, I've learnt to respect my need for *me time,* often undertaking activities to boost my energy. It could be journaling, a walk outdoors, or a relaxation technique such as a body scan. I now know that food does not provide the self-nurturing or *pick-me-up* that my body and mind require. Yet, there are times where I've allowed my energy to become too depleted that adopting any other strategy is a struggle, and I'm perfectly okay with that. These episodes of eating serve as reminders of my need for self-care, *me time* and rest.

Investigate the Thoughts Behind Your Emotions

Although food may be a useful, easily accessible, and socially acceptable way to comfort, distract or numb yourself from the emotions you're feeling, food will not resolve these feelings. Eating may, unfortunately, exacerbate emotional distress by promoting guilt, shame and physical discomfort. Therefore, it is necessary to not only explore other ways to comfort and nurture yourself without food but also explore ways to reduce the intensity of your emotions.

Emotions are feelings derived from how your mind perceives your circumstances, based on your beliefs and past conditioning. Thus, your emotions are a response to how your mind interprets what's occurring in your life, rather than the reality of your circumstances as perceived through your five senses. Your thoughts about what you should or should not eat can also contribute to emotional distress. When you look to food for a distraction from your circumstances, you're not escaping reality, but instead attempting to escape the thoughts in your mind that cause you emotional distress.

To release emotional distress, draw your attention to the sensations in your body right now: the five-sense input occurring in this moment. Your five-sense input is the absolute truth in this moment, not the stories, interpretations, assumptions and worst-case scenarios your mind has conjured up.

A practice of sensing *what is* or eating with your full awareness can assist in quietening your mind and tuning into your senses. Beyond these practices, it is still necessary to investigate the thoughts that cause you emotional distress and potentially lead to emotional eating.

Mind your thoughts

Your thoughts create your reality: your emotional state in the moment is founded on the meaning you give to the content of the moment. Any thoughts of what should or should not have happened in the past or future— interpretations, assumptions and perceived consequences—all have the power to create physical responses and emotional charge in your body.

However, your thoughts can fool you. They can create the illusion that you can change what has already happened or what will happen, just by thinking. You cannot, and believing so only serves to generate emotional distress, such as worry, nervousness and anxiety.

In no way am I implying that undesirable events and emotions will not occur in your life. Some situations and events will cause anger, sadness and elation. However, the emotional distress I'm referring to is that which is self-inflicted as a result of your thoughts and your attempts to control the situation, rather than accept *what is*.

Let me explain. Say you've overeaten, gained weight, not succeeded on a diet or ate a snack that was not permitted on your meal plan. Rather than being truly present with *what is* and drawing your awareness to the physical sensations in your body, you instead start to interpret the situation and behaviours. You may consider: *what does this mean about me, them, my future and my self-worth?* You consider why this happened and what should or shouldn't have happened. You consider what the consequences of this happening might be. You may experience a barrage of thoughts that compound one another. Let me illustrate this with an imaginary scenario.

Imagine you're at work. You head to the tearoom, where you discover your colleague, Judy, has made a delicious looking cake. Judy offers you a slice. You can't say no because that would be rude, and you don't want to offend her. Hence, it's Judy's fault that you're eating the cake, not yours. You use this reasoning to justify your desire for eating the cake, rather than consider it as your lack of self-control.

You break off a piece of cake from the slice Judy gave you and place it into your mouth. It's crumbly but moist. It seems to melt in your mouth with minimal chewing. You are having a *moment* with that piece of cake.

Then Judy pipes up, 'Oh, I'm so pleased you're enjoying the cake. I was a little uncertain about the two cups of sugar and one cup of olive oil, but it has turned out all right, don't you think?' Your mind kicks in, *You what? How many cups of sugar? What were you thinking? Are you trying to sabotage my diet? Just because you're fat, doesn't mean you have to make me fat also.* You again consider that you only ate the cake because it was there and wanted to make Judy happy.

Your thoughts about what you or Judy should or shouldn't have done have replaced the pleasurable moment of eating cake. You are no longer aware of the five-sense experience of eating cake but what the future consequences of eating this cake will be, and how Judy and your other work colleagues will judge you. You can no longer enjoy the cake; you despise it as much as you now despise Judy.

As a consequence of this experience, how do you think you'll treat Judy in the future? How do you think you'll respond to her future gestures of kindness? You might interpret her actions with your preconceived notions that she's inconsiderate and vindictive. However, all Judy did was express her generosity and joy of baking.

Nonetheless, your mind has now made an enemy of the cake, of Judy and of yourself. No longer are you enjoying a blissful moment of eating cake and the company of a caring colleague. Instead, you're feeling stressed, annoyed, guilty, ashamed, stupid, and any number of other negative emotions.

In this story, the cake was always innocent, as Judy most likely was also. It was the thoughts and stories you potentially attached to the cake and to Judy's actions that led to the negative emotions you felt. Rather than blaming the cake, its maker or yourself, would it not be more productive and less emotionally distressing to investigate the thoughts that take you out of the moment of enjoying cake? Remember, it's not the situation but your thoughts about the situation or a person's behaviour that causes you emotional distress.

Investigate your thoughts for truth

The process I use for investigating your thoughts for truth is derived from the book, *Loving What Is,* by Byron Katie and adapted by Michelle Stanton in her book, *The Timeless World.* Michelle terms the tool for investigating your thoughts for truth, *debunking.*

The process of *debunking* involves investigating your thoughts and beliefs surrounding a specific situation or behaviour that caused your emotional distress for truth. Firstly, you notice how the situation or behaviour made you feel. You then record your assumptions, interpretations, conclusions, rules and consequences of this situation or behaviour. Sometimes the thoughts you record can seem ridiculous or petty. However, if they come to mind, they are likely to play a role in how you interpret certain situations and behaviours.

Once you've recorded all the thoughts associated with a specific situation or behaviour, you then investigate the beliefs for truth one at a time, by asking yourself the following questions:

1. Is it true?
2. Can I absolutely know it's true?
3. How do I react when I believe this thought?
4. How would I be without this thought?
5. Is it worth hanging onto this belief? Accept *what is*.

The first two questions can help you to see that many of your thoughts are either not true or you cannot know whether they are true or not. The last three questions essentially ask whether the thoughts serve you in any way. These questions can help you to let go of the thoughts that take you out of the moment and cause you emotional distress.

Not only this, letting go of the underlying beliefs can influence how you think, feel and behave, and thus experience your life. It can influence how you respond to others, as your actions are then based on the reality of the moment rather than the stories your mind has made up. Once you work through these questions for a variety of situations and behaviours, you'll likely become more proficient at asking yourself these questions as you go about your day.

You can use the process of debunking to explore your reasons for emotional eating in the absence of physical hunger, or why you feel emotional distress as a consequence of your eating. In the scenario of Judy sharing cake with you at your workplace, the mere eating of cake does not cause emotional distress. Emotional distress is the result of your thoughts. So, let's debunk them.

✍ Debunk your sabotaging thoughts

You can debunk any situation or behaviour that causes you emotional distress. To do so, write your response to each of the below statements in your Workbook or journal:

- *I feel* (describe your feelings in as much detail as you can)
- *Because* (write down the facts, not your assumptions or interpretations)
- *I think this happened because* (your assumptions) *and this means* (your interpretations and conclusions)
- *What SHOULD or SHOULD NOT have happened* (which of your rules have been broken)?
- *The consequences are* (what's the worst thing that could happen as a result of this)?

Write down everything that comes to mind, no matter how ridiculous or petty it may seem. Once you've completed your responses associated with the specific situation or behaviour, investigate each statement by asking yourself the following questions in turn:

1. Is it true?
2. Can I absolutely know it's true?
3. How do I react when I believe this thought?
4. How would I be without this thought?
5. Is it worth hanging onto this belief? Accept *what is.*

Debunking Example: the 'Inconsiderate' Colleague

Let's use the debunking tool together. Imagine my colleague asked me to do him a favour: send an email. I felt obliged to do it as I didn't want to create conflict in the office and I tend to want to please others.

cont.

Despite my action, inside I am fuming. I feel annoyed because I believe my colleague should have seen that I was busy and didn't have the time to do him a favour. I feel underappreciated and gutless, as I should have stood up for myself. I feel like taking time out for a chocolate break but feel so overwhelmed by my workload that I instead devour the stale crackers I found in my office desk drawer. To debunk this situation, I would write my responses to each of the debunking statements:

I feel (describe your feelings in as much detail as you can)

Annoyed, disappointed, worthless.

Because (write down the facts, not your assumptions or interpretations)

My colleague asked me to email the accounts to head office.

I think this happened because (your assumptions) and this means (your interpretations and conclusions)

My colleague doesn't understand how busy I am.
My colleague doesn't think I have enough work to do.
My colleague thinks his job is more important than mine.
My colleague is arrogant and demanding.
My colleague doesn't acknowledge the work that I do.
My colleague is not understanding and has unrealistic expectations.

What SHOULD or SHOULD NOT have happened (which of your rules have been broken)?

My colleague should have sent the email himself.
My colleague should have seen how busy I was.
My colleague should not assume I have more time available than him.
My colleague should not ask for favours when I'm busy and already falling behind in my work.

cont.

My colleague should not ask me to do tasks that he really should do himself.
I should have told him to send the email himself.
I should stand up for what I believe in, and myself.
I should not allow people to persuade me to do things that aren't my responsibility.

The consequences are (what's the worst thing that could happen as a result of this)?

I could create an enemy at work.
I might be seen as unreasonable by other colleagues.
I'd be embarrassed to ask a favour from anyone at work if I made a big deal out of it.
I would dread going to work.
I could lose my job.
I'd struggle to pay the bills.
I'd look like a failure to my friends and family.

I hope the above example illustrates how many thoughts can arise from one action. Now I'd take one thought at a time and investigate it for truth. Let's take the first statement: ***My colleague doesn't understand how busy I am.***

1. Is it true?

No, we all have a lot to do at work.

Yet I may still have resistance to letting this thought go as I feel he should not have asked me.

2. Can I absolutely know it's true?

No. I can't absolutely know what he should or should not have done. I don't know what is going on for him. He too is perhaps distracted and stressed.

cont.

3. How do I react when I believe this thought?

It makes me feel annoyed, tense, and angry.

4. How would I be without this thought?

I'd feel peaceful and calm, whether I sent the email or not.

5. Is it worth hanging onto this belief? Accept *what is*.

No, it just causes me emotional distress.

To fully debunk the situation, work through each thought, one at a time. It may seem tedious and drawn out, yet you may have to work through the debunking process multiple times before it *sinks in*. It's not a matter of doing this once and everything will resolve itself. In life, you'll experience many situations and people that challenge your belief system and cause emotional distress. The same issue may arise multiple times, which means that it's necessary to investigate your beliefs further.

Investigating your beliefs for truth does not imply inaction; rather, it enables you to diffuse the emotional charge associated with a situation. In the above example, I may still talk to my colleague about the best approach to deal with priorities or requests. However, having debunked the situation, I'd be better able to approach this conversation calmly and with a clarity of *what is* rather than with what I perceive to have or should have happened.

I encourage you to practise the process of debunking, starting with issues that are bothering you in any aspect of your life. Then consider your beliefs about your body, food and weight. You could debunk a situation or behaviour that has caused you emotional distress in the past few days, or you could try debunking one of the statements you recorded in one of the Self-Reflection Activities completed earlier, such as resistance to change, food labels and food rules.

cont.

Debunking some of the thoughts you've recorded in the previous activities may help to shift any beliefs that might sabotage you. For instance, if you recorded that you would feel guilt or shame for eating a doughnut, you could debunk it. Let's give it a go with an example.

Debunking Example: Guilty Doughnut Eating

I feel (describe your feelings in as much detail as you can)

Guilty and ashamed.

Because (write down the facts, not your assumptions or interpretations)

I ate a doughnut.

I think this happened because (your assumptions) and this means (your interpretations and conclusions)

I am weak, pathetic, useless.
I have no self-control.
I have no self-respect.

What SHOULD or SHOULD NOT have happened (which of your rules have been broken)?

I should not have eaten the doughnut.
I should have had more self-control.
I should prioritise eating healthily.

The consequences are (what's the worst thing that could happen as a result of this)?

I'll feel bloated.
I'll get fat.
I'll never achieve a body with which I am happy.
I'll always be unhealthy.
I'll remain single and unlovable.

cont.

I'll get diabetes and die.

To debunk your food labels and rules, you could write down all your responses for a few items of food and drink. Once you've recorded your thoughts, then investigate the statements for truth. If a statement presents multiple times, such as, *I will get fat*, or *I will always be unhealthy*, you may only need to investigate that statement one time.

Let's explore this with one of the example statements above: ***I should prioritise eating healthily.***

1.   Is it true?

Of course, I should prioritise eating healthy, without my health what do I have?

2.   Can I absolutely know it's true?

No, I can't absolutely know with one hundred percent certainty that my health is my greatest priority in this moment. I have other priorities and responsibilities in my life, and although I value my health, it's not necessarily my greatest priority in this moment.

3.   How do I react when I believe this thought?

Although I ate the doughnut while enjoying the company of friends, when I think the thought that I should prioritise eating healthily it causes me to feel anxious and stressed. I feel conflicted and find it hard to stay present in the moment and truly enjoy their company. I'm distracted and short with them.

4.   How would I be without this thought?

I'd be relaxed around food and enjoy the food and company.

5.   Is it worth hanging onto this belief? Accept *what is*.

No, it just takes me out of the moment and causes me emotional distress.

cont.

You might do the above only a few times with several of the foods you identified labels and rules for, continuing this process until you feel you're creating a shift in how you think about food and drink. You could also come back to this when you feel emotionally distressed as a consequence of what you've eaten or your eating behaviour.

Reframe Your Thinking

Not only can you use how you feel to identify when you're telling yourself *stories*, but you can also observe the language you use when you speak to others about yourself or your internal self-talk. Your internal dialogue can influence how you see the world, as you perceive the world through the lens of your thoughts.

✍ Reframe your thinking

Observe the words you use when you describe your circumstances, aspirations, ideas and yourself. When you use words such as *never* or *always,* you're implying the situation is absolute, rather than circumstantial. When you use words such as *need, must* or *should,* you're imposing pressure on yourself and not providing room for going off-course or failing. Reflect on whether you use any of the below words or phrases.

Word or Phrase	Underlying Belief
I *should* or I *shouldn't…*	You are resisting reality and believing the rules (and I don't mean the law) to be an absolute truth, rather than *what is* in the moment.
I *must* or I *mustn't…*; I *have to…*; I *need to…*	There's an assumption that you know what's required—the steps, plan, strategy, right approach—to achieve your desired goal or outcome. And you are attached to achieving the end goal.

cont.

I *can't*; I don't know if I *can*; I *couldn't*…	Without trying, how do you know if you can or can't? Even if you've tried a hundred times, how do you know that trying one more time will not achieve success? Anyway, perhaps joy is not in success but in the trying.
If this happens, then…	You're concerning yourself with the unknown; thinking about *what ifs* does more to generate worry than serve you to deal with the situation. When *it* happens, it happens. When it happens, you will deal with it.
It's *too* hard…	The word *too* implies that it is essentially impossible. You are either setting yourself up for failure, to give up when the going gets tough, or to push yourself so hard that there is no longer joy in the unfolding of *what is*.
Only when this happens, will I…	Who is in control of your life? If your actions are conditional on certain feedback, then although it can feel you are handing control over to the *universe* or God, you are attempting to control *what is* by not taking action.
One day I'd like…	Ask yourself, why not now? What are you afraid of? What do you believe needs to be in place before you can start? Are these stories true?
I don't deserve…	Who says you have to earn anything to pursue your passions or dreams? Why don't you deserve what others do?
Who am I to…	How are you any different from any other person that has spoken out or pursued their dreams?
I'm not worth it…	Who says? Worthy for what? Do you have to earn happiness?
When I'm… then I'll…	You've made your actions conditional. Ask yourself is this a true limitation or something your mind has made up.
I *never*…	Is it true in every situation and relationship?
	cont.

I *always*...	If you think *I always say stupid things*, is that absolutely true, always? No, the thought is possibly only based on one experience (or a select number of experiences). It is not absolute.
I'm not going to succeed, so why bother?	How do you know? You are setting yourself up for failure before you begin and closing yourself off from endless possibility and joy.

Take note of what words and phrases you commonly use and reflect on why. You may choose to consciously try to refrain from using a specific word or phrase for a period and then move onto another word or phrase. Or you may choose to debunk the thoughts associated with use of these words.

Fuelling Your Emotions

At times, you might use food to fuel your emotions, to increase the feeling of pleasure or pain through your food choices, eating behaviour and sheer volume of food. In this respect, it's not the food itself but the way you use food that contributes to a negative association. Nonetheless, there may be certain foods that can enhance feelings of pleasure or pain, beyond the volume you eat. Hence it can be useful to identify foods that impact you emotionally, so that you can be more conscious of their consumption.

Joyful Eating Principle 6.
FEED YOUR SOUL

Rather than judge yourself for eating for emotional reasons,
explore the emotions that trigger you to eat, and identify ways
to cope with your emotions without food wherever possible.

15

Find Your Own Way to Nourish Your Body and Mind

"The intent of learning about nutrition isn't to perfect your diet. It simply provides information to consider in your decisions about what to eat."

—Michelle May MD

If you've struggled with your weight or found it hard to sustain a balanced diet, the countless solutions that promise to enable you to achieve the body you desire can be captivating. It can be appealing to have your diet simplified, to be provided with an exact prescription of how to eat, or to find a concoction, such as a meal replacement or bar that meets all your nutritional needs.

The problem is, *no-one* has the answer as to the *right* way to eat. Your body can acquire the energy and nutrition it requires through many food combinations. So long as you obtain the essential requirements of vitamins, minerals, glucose (sugars), amino acids (proteins), and fats (essential fatty acids) that your body requires to regenerate and function, you have ample scope for flexibility in your diet.

There simply isn't a one-size-fits-all diet, as everyone is unique. Biologically you have unique genetics, rate of digestion, gut microbiota and metabolism. Overlaid on your biology is your unique past conditioning, upbringing and family history, stress levels, food preferences, food associations, cultural and societal norms, religious beliefs and practices, environmental influences, relationships, work, socioeconomics and your local community.

Moreover, I'd hazard a guess that it's not a lack of nutrition knowledge that sabotages your eating. Although a basic knowledge of nutrition is beneficial, it's more likely that you, like most people, are confused and overwhelmed by the excess of contradictory information on diet. You may be uncertain how to put this information into practise. Or you may find that other factors influence your eating decisions and behaviours. Let's end the search for the *right* way to eat, so that you can forge your own unique path to nourish your body.

Abiding by Dietary Guidelines

Most government health organisations provide dietary guidelines based on the most up-to-date scientific evidence. Dietary guidelines are periodically updated as scientists continue to discover more about how the body works and responds to dietary intake. Hence, dietary guidelines are only as accurate as the scientific evidence available to date: they are not absolute.

Some popular diet proponents dispute government-created dietary guidelines, declaring that they're too generic or not substantial enough to create a significant shift in your health. Dietary guidelines can seem inflexible with regard to individuals that have dietary constraints due to allergies, food intolerance, genetic disorders, specific food preferences or religious beliefs.

Basically, the guidelines provide dietary recommendations for healthy individuals at a population level, based on the food preferences of that population. They are not tailored to an individual's health conditions, preferences, culture or social differences. This does not mean that they're not valuable, but that any specific requirements or modifications need to be devised yourself or with the assistance of a nutrition professional.

Popular diets are not the answer to the concerns with government dietary guidelines, either. Many popular diets are even less flexible than the government dietary guidelines they refute. Some eliminate entire food groups and provide extensive lists of *yes* or *no* foods. They can be convincing, drawing on selective scientific and anecdotal evidence. Yet in all likelihood, they are less scientifically rigorous than the dietary guidelines they attempt to replace.

Popular diet proponents may be adamant that the diet they developed sculpted their body and reversed numerous ailments. However, this may not be the case for you: what worked for them to lose weight or reverse allegedly incurable diseases may not hold true for you. Once you acknowledge your uniqueness and accept dietary guidelines (or any diet), as just that, guidelines, you can free yourself to explore a way of eating that suits your body, preferences and lifestyle.

✍ Your perception of dietary guidelines and advice

In this activity, I invite you to look over some general dietary guidelines widely agreed upon in the scientific literature and public health sector. Consider the thoughts or emotions that arise for you.

General Dietary Guidelines[1]

1. Drink plenty of water.
2. Enjoy a variety of fruits.
3. Eat plenty of vegetables, including different types, colours, and legumes, like peas, chickpeas, beans and lentils.
4. Choose mostly wholegrain cereal foods.
5. Consume a range of proteins, such as lean meats, poultry, fish, eggs, tofu, nuts and seeds, and legumes.
6. Limit your intake of foods containing saturated fat, trans fats, processed meats, added salt, added sugars and alcohol.
7. For fats, choose foods containing predominantly monounsaturated and polyunsaturated fats, such as olive oil, spreads, nut butters and avocado.
8. Consume discretionary foods and drinks, such as processed meats, cakes, biscuits, chips, commercial burgers, pizzas, fried foods and alcohol only occasionally and in small quantities.

Record your perception of dietary guidelines in your Workbook or journal. Then consider the below questions to explore your perception further:

*   Where do you meet, exceed or fall short of the dietary guidelines?
*   In what ways do you feel that you could improve your nutritional intake?

cont.

---

[1]   Please note: the above dietary guidelines are a generic representation. More specific guidelines can be sourced from the relevant health organisation in your country.

- What are barriers to you meeting dietary guidelines or improving your nutritional intake?
- What are some perceptions or associations with these dietary guidelines that you feel prevent you from embracing them?
- What do you believe to be conflicting desires or values that may prevent you from meeting the dietary guidelines?
- Do you experience judgemental thoughts about yourself with regards to these guidelines? How does this make you feel?
- What additional details or evidence do you feel you require in order to adopt dietary guidelines or any other intake recommendations?

You don't need to record a response to each of the above questions. That said, I encourage you to take the time to consider whether you feel resistance or challenges to meeting basic dietary requirements. These might be a consequence of your own thinking or behaviour, or external influences, such as contradictory information or social pressures.

Devising Your Own Diet

Nutritional guidelines, or in fact any dietary recommendations, provide a rough guide that you can tweak to suit your body and lifestyle. You can do this through observing how your body responds to the foods you eat. Let me explain with the example of protein.

Protein has become a champion in many popular diets. Yet, science fails to demonstrate that any specific apportioning of carbohydrates, protein and fat (within the recommended intake of total energy and essential nutrients) is better than another for either weight loss or health.

An alternative to following a diet precisely is to focus on what feels good to your body and provides you with sustained energy throughout the day. For instance, if you start your day with a predominantly refined carbohydrate breakfast and find your energy flailing by 10 am, you could adjust your breakfast to include more complex carbohydrates, protein or fat.

Scientific evidence can be useful in helping you to identify foods or lifestyle behaviours that you would like to explore. However, rather than forcing it or feeling like a failure if you don't stick to the change, you could instead focus on exploring whether you enjoy the change and notice how your body responds to it. In this way, dietary guidelines and associated recipe books can inspire you to try new foods or incorporate more variety into your diet, rather than being something you follow precisely. Banish any thought that a diet is *right* and that you or your body is not.

If you enjoy learning about new foods and trying new recipes, I encourage you to do so in this explorative way. It can, however, become problematic when you're constantly looking outside of yourself for the answers on how to eat, and when you put more faith in others' recommendations and programs. Do explore new foods if you're so inclined, but assess them for truth for you, based on what you enjoy and feels good to your body.

Furthermore, be aware that change to your way of eating may not always feel great to start with. For example, increasing fibre intake can lead to bloating, gas and intestinal discomfort if your diet was substantially low in fibre. It doesn't mean that fibre isn't good for your body, but that a gentler and more gradual introduction is required. Guidance from a suitably qualified nutrition professional can be helpful. If you don't have a health condition, it can be useful to begin to *listen* to your body before investigating recommendations and advice.

Intuitive Eating

A preschool-aged child can eat part of a sandwich and then go about playing without finishing it. They don't consider whether they'll feel hungry later or worry about the waste. They eat when they're hungry, and stop when they're not.

Scientific research confirms that young children intuitively know what and how to eat. A study in the 1930s of preschool-aged orphans who were provided with a constantly available selection of wholefoods, such as wholegrains, vegetables, fruit, milk and meats, found that the children's diets, although not nutritionally balanced at each meal, overall provided all the vitamins, minerals and amino acids required for healthy growth (98,99).

A component of learning to eat intuitively is engaging all the senses in the process of eating, like the conscious eating practice. On first being introduced to a food, a child can require up to fifteen exposures to that specific food to establish a liking for it (100). These exposures provide the opportunity for a child to become familiar with the smell, taste and texture of food, through playing with their food. This playing can include sucking and chewing food, and at times spitting it out before proceeding with another *taste test*.

Unfortunately, these behaviours can be frustrating to a parent who wishes that their child would simply put food in their mouth and eat. This frustration can potentially lead a parent to give up on providing their child with a specific food. In other circumstances, a parent may force their child to eat food that they don't enjoy because of its nutritional value. When a child is pressured to eat a certain food, say broccoli, it may actually reduce their intake of that food and initiate a disliking for it. In contrast, when food is used as a reward, it can increase the liking of this *reward* food and decrease the liking of the *means* food. So, when a parent tells their child, 'if you eat all your broccoli you can have ice cream', it reinforces a perception that the means food, in this case, broccoli, is bad or yuk and that the reward food, ice cream, is good or yummy.

As a child, you too may have learnt that if you eat a certain way, you can make others happy. Conversely, you may have learnt that if you kick up a fuss or create a substantial enough mess, you'd be given the foods you really wanted to eat. These early eating experiences can reinforce beliefs and behaviours concerning food that you carry through into adulthood.

Trust Your Body

You might now be wondering how you can go about restoring trust in your body and yourself around food. Let me begin by defining what trust is.

Trust originates from a belief or confidence in someone or something. So that even if they *stuff up* in some way, or don't behave as you'd expected, you give them the benefit of the doubt. The same is true of your body. Despite your body perhaps exhibiting signs that it's not working to the best of its ability, this does not mean that it is untrustworthy.

Sickness, weight loss or gain, aches and pains, fatigue and digestive issues are signs that something is *out of balance* and requires your attention. Unless there is an underlying genetic disorder, your body functions to maintain balance given the external stimuli, whether that be food, foreign substances, injury, or physical or emotional trauma. For example, an increase in blood pressure serves a beneficial role in helping you to deal with stress or avert danger. Inflammation helps to defend and protect your body from foreign substances at sites of injury or infection. Although elevated blood pressure and chronic inflammation can contribute to serious and debilitating health conditions, they are generally the result of your body functioning to maintain balance, and not a sign that your body is broken.

In fact, your body is an incredible organism capable of taking breath, pumping oxygen and millions of other functions without your conscious effort. If you experience health concerns that are mild or non-life threatening, you can adopt lifestyle changes to help reinstate balance. However, beware that the intention is not to self-diagnose but to recognise when your body alerts you to a need for movement, relaxation, sleep, nourishment or other forms of self-care.

Signs that your body is out of balance don't necessarily mean that you need to avoid or eliminate associated foods. Instead, investigate why your body is out of balance. On occasion, you may believe that you are *listening* to your body's signals and interpreting them correctly, without realising how proclaimed negative health effects of certain foods influence your perception that *they're* the cause of your body being out of balance. Thus, you may not read your body's signals with complete impartiality. For instance, the popularity of gluten-free diets has led many people to believe that they are gluten intolerant. I confess I was one of them!

Another challenge is that you may ignore your body's signals or have forgotten what *normal* feels like all together. You may be too busy or stressed to take notice of your body. You may feel so overwhelmed with other responsibilities that you don't have the energy to deal with health concerns. Perhaps you fear the diagnosis or actions that will be required.

Trust takes time. Give yourself time to become more aware of your body, your hunger and fullness cues, and to embrace conscious eating. It is through developing these skills that you will be better able to notice subtleties in your body and its response to the food you eat and other lifestyle behaviours.

It may be difficult to accurately interpret your body's signals if you have been in the habit of covering them up, such as combating tiredness with coffee or headaches with painkillers. Overriding your body's signals is not always a problem. For example, if you're in so much pain that you cannot move, painkillers may be advantageous in getting you up and moving again. They may be better for your healing and recovery than being bedridden. However, it is important to acknowledge that certain behaviours can dampen your body's signals and result in you not addressing what is out of balance.

In a similar vein, if your health concerns are causing you considerable discomfort, are persistent and recurrent, or your body is not functioning as it normally does, you may require specialised nutritional or medical support. Likewise, if your health concerns or associated medications alter your body signals, such as hunger or pain receptors, or you have certain health conditions that mandate specific dietary considerations, you likely require support. Needing assistance in deciphering your body's signals doesn't mean that you have failed in some way.

Although the intention of tuning into your body is to eat and move in ways that enable you to feel your best, you don't control how your body responds to external stimuli. Some days you may feel tired because you were kept awake by a crying baby, noisy neighbours or something else that required your attention. Other days you may feel bloated because the only food available at a meeting was deep-fried finger food, and you were hungry. The intent is not to feel good all of the time, but to prioritise feeling good in each moment through the actions you take.

End Counting Calories and Portion Control

Many diets and meal plans call for you to measure and count your intake in some way. Eating prescribed portions can erode your ability to *listen* to and honour your hunger signals, as you eat to portion sizes indicated on a package or meal plan, not to your hunger and fullness cues.

If you've eaten in a portion-controlled way in the past, you may feel anxious to stop eating to pre-set portions. I've had people tell me that they've done a weight loss program multiple times with companies that provide all their meals or meal replacements. Because every time they've come off the program they've put on weight, they're now afraid of preparing their own food where they have to control their portions. It can take time to establish balance in your eating and trust in your body.

If eating excessively or mindlessly has been an issue for you, you may find that becoming acquainted with portion sizes can provide a guide for *listening* to your body. In this way, rather than confining your intake to the recommended portion sizes, observe with curiosity how suggested portions *feel* to your body. You may, for example, eat the portion recommended on a package and then tune into your body to assess how this quantity *feels*. You may then decide whether you would like to eat more, eat another food, or stop eating.

Alternatively, you may find that you need to ignore portion sizes as you learn to tune into your body. Through self-investigation and awareness of your body, you can determine portions of specific foods that sufficiently sustain you.

To Meal Plan or Not?

Some bloggers and nutritionists suggest that a sure-fire way to eat healthily is to meal plan. However, if weekly meal planning or having a preparation day doesn't suit your personality and lifestyle, or you cringe at the idea of being that prepared, you don't have to adopt what worked for someone else. Honour your uniqueness. There is no right or wrong way to set yourself up for nutritionally balanced eating. Meal planning also doesn't guarantee healthy eating, as many people who've attempted rigid diets can attest!

Meal plans are generally quite limited in that they are often a prescription of eating for only one day or week. If followed long-term, meal plans can limit the variety of foods you consume, which can have nutritional implications as well as cause disinterest and boredom in your meals. Boredom with eating can cause you to *break* a diet, even if it provides sufficient energy.

Furthermore, meal planning with set recipes often does not consider unexpected life events or account for how hungry you may or may not be when it's mealtime. Therefore, if you choose to plan meals ahead, keep it flexible, and remember that your plans are only your best guess in the moment.

At this point, it could be valuable to investigate what are either facilitators or inhibitors of balanced eating for you, such as creativity in the kitchen, time to prepare food, cooking skills, motivation to cook, or your perceived worthiness of delicious and nourishing foods.

Let's say you don't enjoy preparing food. Explore this, considering whether you're afraid of making a mess you have to clean up later. Or maybe you're afraid of having a meal fail and feeling like a failure, of being judged or wasting food. Consider whether you enjoy being spontaneous and having a selection of meats (or alternative proteins) and vegetables available so that you can tap into your intuition and creativity... or whether this lack of planning evokes anxiety for you? Do you feel too distracted or stressed to even think about preparing food? Through this exploration, you can gain clarity on what will serve you best for creating healthful food choices and eating behaviours.

An alternative to meal planning could be to develop a list of meals and snacks that you enjoy and feel good to your body. You could put together a list in your Workbook, journal or dedicate a folder for recipes. You could then use it for inspiration at times when you can't think of what to eat or feel your eating has become monotonous.

Whatever way you wish to approach meal preparation, ensure it's not a source of stress and anxiety for you. Nor should it erode trust in your body. The approach you adopt ought to enable you to enjoy a wide variety of foods and nourish your body in a balanced way. One person may find meal planning stress-provoking. Another may find it useful to follow or develop a meal plan for the week ahead to reduce the stress and anxiety of not knowing what to eat each day.

You may find that establishing a routine is beneficial to start with if your eating has been sporadic, or you haven't been obtaining sufficient nourishment. Establishing regular eating patterns may enable you to eat consciously and draw your awareness to your body… so that you can eventually become more relaxed and intuitive in your eating.

Opt for Variety

Eating a variety of fresh produce, wholegrains and minimally processed foods can increase the likelihood of supplying your body with the full spectrum of vitamins and minerals it requires. If you find yourself on autopilot with your shopping and meal preparation, or in a rut with your diet, it may be worth considering how to increase variety in your diet.

Exploring ways to enjoy more variety can be useful not only to help increase the nutrition you supply your body, but it can also reignite enjoyment of foods you may have long forgotten, or have avoided because of a perceived disliking. For example, you mightn't have enjoyed mushy peas as a child. However, by venturing to try them prepared in different ways, you may discover you enjoy peas when fresh from the pod, or combined in soups or fritters. Alternatively, you may have a limited repertoire of how to prepare a certain vegetable and it's become boring to you. Yet, there are many other ways you can prepare any food to arouse more pleasure and enjoyment.

✍ Explore a variety of nourishing foods

This activity is intended to increase the variety of fruits and vegetables in your diet, discover ways you can prepare them, and to potentially rekindle enjoyment of a food you believe you dislike. This activity is not about eating foods that you absolutely can't stand, but rather, giving foods a try, in a variety of ways, and seeing whether you do enjoy them.

Purchase it

Similar to the scene in the movie, *City of Angels*, as described in the section, *Conscious Eating*, I'd like you to head to a fruit and vegetable store or local market and spend some time checking out the produce. Take some time to explore what's on offer, rather than rush around grabbing your usual fruits and vegetables. Take some time to look at the variety of shapes, colours and textures. Like in the movie, take the time to touch, feel or smell different produce. Then choose something that appeals to you that you don't normally purchase in your weekly shop.

Prepare it

Take the item home and consider how you may like to prepare it. You may have prepared it before in ways you've enjoyed, or you may never have. If you're unsure how to prepare it or would like to consider alternative ways to prepare it than you usually do, you may like to do some research online for side or main dish recipes. Alternatively, you may like to prepare it on its own to really taste the fruit or vegetable, possibly having it raw, steamed, baked or sautéed and combined with yogurt, olive oil, butter, salt and pepper, lemon juice, herbs, spices or another type of dressing and seasoning you enjoy.

cont.

Consume it

When you consume the item or dish you've prepared, do so consciously. Observe the colour, shape, texture and sound as you bite into and chew it. Notice the sensations on your tongue and how the texture changes as you chew. Discern the taste, and notice how it changes from your first bite to your last chew, and before you swallow.

Take the time to experience the food without labelling it as good or bad, like or dislike. Take in the sensory experience as if you were examining it so that you could later recall it to a detective who has no idea what the food is. You could describe the food to yourself in your mind, or you may like to do this as a family and each describe the food to one another. Playing food detective, rather than food police, can be a great way for the whole family to explore how they experience food and become more adventurous and inquisitive in eating.

Contemplate it

After this experience, take the time to reflect on what you learnt about your selection of fruits and vegetables, or creativity in the kitchen. Maybe your chosen vegetable has withered to an inedible, unidentifiable object in the bottom of your crisper. Maybe you rediscovered you enjoy a vegetable you'd long forgotten. You may have enjoyed the challenge of devising a recipe from a new or irregularly consumed vegetable. Or perhaps you discovered that preparing a wider variety requires more planning and consideration, such as a cooking class or recipes to follow.

If you discovered that you'd like more meal planning, you could take a similar approach to this activity and choose one recipe a week from a website, magazine or book in order to increase the repertoire of dishes you prepare. Taking an incremental approach is far less overwhelming and more likely to create long-term change than adopting an entirely new meal plan. You may like to keep an online file of successful recipes, a Pinterest board or a loose-leaf folder; depending on the way you like to access your recipe inspiration.

Ignite a Love of Wholefoods

The health benefits of eating predominantly wholefoods has become increasingly well-known. Unfortunately, this has resulted in wholefood *diets*, which have many of the same downfalls as weight loss diets. Many wholefood diets advocate for specific proportions of macronutrients and dictate what and when you should or should not eat. Some declare that certain foods are bad—or even *poison*.

Although increasing wholefood consumption and reducing refined, highly-processed and nutritionally devoid foods is health promoting, there is no exact formula for enduring health. In support of this, a recent study found that when individuals switched to low processed and low glycaemic foods, the proportions of macronutrients had little bearing on the weight loss achieved (101). The study demonstrated that weight loss by overweight men was the same whether they undertook a very high-fat, low-carbohydrate diet or a low-fat, high-carbohydrate diet, when total calorie, essential fatty acid and protein intake was held constant. Although there is a difference in the quality of the foods you can choose, proclaiming a specific macronutrient apportioning as more health-promoting than another is scientifically unfounded (102). Eating a variety of unprocessed wholefoods, such as fruit, vegetables, meats, nuts and seeds, and minimally refined or processed foods, such as oils, grains, legumes and dairy-products, is more important than focusing on proportions of macronutrients.

Furthermore, consuming a diet dominated by wholefoods may enable you to *listen* to your body more clearly, and assess your most balanced way to eat. A study on young men found that when their consumption of energy-dense foods rich in fat and sugar was increased, they experienced greater *passive* overeating than when consuming wholefoods (103). This passive overeating indicated that there was something other than calorie content influencing the men's consumption, such as the intensity of sweetness, fat content, energy density or other characteristics of highly-processed foods (104). Consistent with this, an animal study that provided a so-called cafeteria (or Western) diet to rats demonstrated that the rats lost *control* of their intake compared to those on a normal chow diet (105).

Despite the health benefits of enjoying a variety of wholefoods, you may find that prioritising unrefined and minimally processed foods continues to feed into diet mentality. If this is the case for you, it may be less stress-provoking to begin by eating all foods without restriction or any preconceived ideas of what is good or bad. You can then begin to explore the wholefoods you enjoy and feel good to your body, taking it at your own pace and in a relaxed way, without eating wholefoods becoming a new *rule* to follow or a source of guilt. All foods have a place in a balanced diet. I know, this sounds like what nutritionists have been saying all along, yet, it's the truth.

There may be certain foods you enjoy that don't make you feel good if you eat them to excess. This doesn't imply that you shouldn't eat them occasionally. If the urge to eat anything arises, whether a whole or refined food, eat it because you really want it, enjoy it, and it feels good to your body. Savour it and taste every mouthful.

Your Body's Response to Specific Foods

Understanding and appreciating how my body responds to food has taught me *what* and *how much* I can eat under certain circumstances. For example, I know that if I've an upcoming presentation that may cause me to feel nervous or anxious, I'm likely to feel bloated and gassy if I consume a large meal beforehand. I've learnt that it's better for me to eat a light meal, if anything, when I feel nervous or anxious, and to eat in as relaxed a state as possible. Likewise, when feeling tired or unmotivated, I used to grab a sugary snack to give me a *lift*. However, it would generally make me feel jittery and panicked. Instead of feeling more alert and focused on my work, I'd feel distracted and scatty. It's through an awareness of how my body responds to specific foods that I've learnt when to eat and when not to eat, and what types of food and in what quantities. Sometimes, when eaten mindfully and in small quantities, the undesirable effects experienced by certain foods will be less pronounced, and can even dissipate entirely.

Similarly for you, a food may cause you to feel out of balance if it creates a change in your mood, energy levels, ability to concentrate, or has physical consequences, such as stomach upsets. The process of learning what foods, in what quantities, and at what times suit your body, requires you to focus on identifying foods that create a feeling of being out of balance. For example, a weekly pizza or a few Saturday night rum-and-cokes may be handled well by your body. However, through understanding your body, you may be aware that you're likely to be *overdoing it* if you combine these foods and drinks with a sugar-laden dessert. Past experience may have demonstrated that this combo doesn't lead to a good night's sleep, or it creates gastrointestinal or energy disturbances the following day. Rather than considering this as *bad*, reflect on what you're doing the following day in making your eating decision. If you want to feel alert and energetic, you may make a different choice than if you're planning a lazy morning in your pyjamas reading a novel (should you be so lucky!)

Through this awareness of your physical, mental and emotional responses to specific foods, you are acquiring the information you need to devise a way of eating that nourishes and sustains you, without it being prescriptive.

If you suspect a food intolerance or suffer from gastrointestinal issues, it's a good idea to seek the counsel of a medical professional in order to rule out any serious health conditions before modifying your intake. You see, if you modify your diet in a way that lessens symptoms but does not resolve them, you could potentially mask a condition that requires specific treatment, beyond food avoidance. Once you know that there is not an underlying health issue, you can then assess how much of these foods and to what frequency feels good for you.

✍ Identify foods that create imbalances for you

Create a list

To better understand the types and quantities of food and drink that suit your body, begin by creating a list of the foods and drinks you would like to investigate. You may choose to investigate foods that are specific to you, such as Oreos, Tim Tams or potato chips, or you may want to focus on macronutrient proportions or general food groupings, such as soft drinks (diet and non-diet), sugary treats, coffee and caffeine, alcohol, foods containing artificial sweeteners, deep-fried foods, and so on.

I admit that these suggestions look a lot like the discretionary food list in government dietary guidelines. However, rather than considering these foods as *bad*, consider how they feel in your body, and develop an understanding of how much and how often you can eat them and feel good. For instance, it is common knowledge that doughnuts are not a health food. When diet mentality predominates, you might restrict doughnuts till you give in and overeat them. Alternatively, you may obsess over doughnuts and eat everything under the sun to avoid eating them. The thing is, one doughnut won't kill you, induce a heart attack or create diabetes. Applying logic, focussing on the health repercussions of eating a doughnut, does little to sway the desire or consumption of them.

That said, if you shift your focus to feeling good, you can choose whether to eat a doughnut (or more than one), based on how it feels in your body. If you consciously eat a doughnut, you may discover that you don't enjoy doughnuts as much as you thought—it was the *forbidden* label that created the appeal. You may find that one doughnut satisfies your craving. You may discover that eating doughnuts when you're relaxed feels better in your body than when you eat while stressed and anxious. When you're stressed (which is when cravings often strike), you may notice that you're more likely to feel bloated, jittery or have a more substantial energy slump, compared to when you're relaxed. Learning how your body responds to a food at

cont.

various times and in various emotional states is substantially different from imposing rules on yourself, such as whether you should or should not eat doughnuts for health reasons or weight concerns.

Get curious

Now that you have a list of foods you wish to investigate, try doing so for one food or drink at a time. Get curious about how your body responds to it. Take note of the physical, mental and emotional signals. You might combine this with your Food and Mood Journal or record your reflections in your Workbook or journal.

Notice variations

Continue investigating your body's response to your chosen food or drink over a period—possibly one week or a month—as it may take some time to notice a consistency in the patterns or variations with time of day, circumstances occurring in your life, your mood and stress levels, phase in your menstrual cycle, and so on. Remember, what may suit you today, might not tomorrow, next month or next year. Some examples of how you could consider patterns are:

• Drinking coffee or soft drink in the morning, afternoon or evening.

• Eating a sugary snack on an empty stomach, after a main meal or when combined with protein and/or fat. Take note of how these differences impact your subsequent hunger, energy levels or desire for more sugary foods.

• Your body's response to coffee or sugar when you are busy, rushed, nervous or anxious.

• How a food feels to your body when eaten slowly versus in a rush.

• Various volumes of certain foods or food combinations.

Through observing patterns, you are not determining what you should or shouldn't eat, but what makes your body and mind feel its best.

Food Cravings

Some mainstream media sites suggest that cravings for food originate from nutritional needs, such as a craving for chips in response to the body's need for certain minerals or salt. This can seem logical. However, this logic falls short when you consider: if your craving is for salt, why don't you crave celery, seaweed or beetroot, which happen to be good sources of sodium? The reason: your *cravings* are not only potentially in response to your requirement for nutrition but from your perception of foods as good or bad, healthy or unhealthy.

Popular media often presents healthy alternatives (or swaps) for commonly desired *unhealthy* foods. Although well intended, these swaps often don't work. If you desire potato chips and a *swap guide* suggests that you eat carrot sticks as an alternative, I'm afraid it doesn't cut it. A *healthy* swap might work if you're eating potato chips on autopilot or haven't considered alternative snack options. But, if you crave potato chips, most of the time only chips will satisfy the craving. I know this is true for me: when I want potato chips, I want potato chips.

As discussed previously, restriction of the foods you desire serves more to amplify your perceived cravings than control them. There have been times when I have wanted chips and denied myself. I might demolish carrot sticks to then find myself searching the cupboard for something else *to hit the spot. How about a rice cake and peanut butter, that's sure to diminish my appetite for crunchy and salty?*

There have been times when, despite attempting swaps and no longer being hungry at all, I have eventually given in to the craving for potato chips. I've had enough experiences like this to know that denying my cravings does not work. So, I've learnt to accept my desire for food and explore it with curiosity, rather than attempting to cover it up, control it, or deny it with carrot sticks, rice cakes or peanut butter. So, rather than resist my food cravings, it's almost as if I welcome them as an opportunity to discover more about why I desire them.

If I eat when I'm not hungry or eat beyond hunger, I now explore why this may be the case, without attempting to change or control it. Say a craving for potato chips arises and I'm not physically hungry, I may then ask myself questions, such as: *Is it the taste and sensory experience of eating chips I desire? Do I feel that I deserve to relax and indulge? Is it that I associate snacking with the TV or the weekend?*

In exploring why I desire potato chips, I can uncover the various reasons for my *cravings*. After this exploration, I may or may not choose to eat chips. If I eat chips, I do so consciously, relishing every last crumb, rather than eating them mindlessly in rapid succession and feeling guilty for the indulgence.

You may be able to explore your cravings when they strike, as I have described above, or you may have to wait until later to reflect on an eating occurrence. The intention is not to reduce or control your eating, but to understand *why* you desire certain foods and explore what you truly require to feel balanced: physically, mentally and emotionally. The thing is, your desire for food and perceived cravings involve a complicated interplay of nutritional requirements, desire, associations, mood, stress and so on. It is not as simple as a healthy food swap.

When you first allow yourself to eat without restriction, you may initially eat the foods you desire with gleeful abandon. This possible overeating or compulsive eating is likely to subside as you begin to eat to your hunger and your body's cues, rather than rules and labels. Once you no longer restrict foods that you've perceived as unhealthy or forbidden, you may find that their insatiable appeal dissipates.

> Once you no longer restrict foods that you've perceived as unhealthy or forbidden, you may find that their insatiable appeal dissipates.

You may find this hard to believe if your current *cravings* feel intense. However, your desire for certain foods is likely to be amplified by perceived pleasure, anticipated restriction, or rebellion, rather than a true liking. Research has shown that *perceived* pleasure is greater for foods that are restricted, irrespective of liking for that food (40). So, it's not your liking of food but the restriction that causes cravings and *addictive-like* eating behaviour (106).

Despite the popularity of a food addiction theory, there is insufficient scientific evidence to suggest that there are addictive properties of foods. It may feel like it is impossible to control yourself around certain foods. However, unlike addictive substances where an addict requires larger doses to experience an effect, and requires the substance to prevent withdrawal symptoms, food doesn't have the same physiological effect on the body (107). Further, unlike an addiction to drugs or alcohol, which is often treated with abstinence, the same is not possible with food. Therefore, rather than demonising certain foods, or attempting abstinence of foods you crave or eat uncontrollably, I believe it is more beneficial to focus on the beliefs and behaviours associated with certain foods in order to reduce the cravings and addictive-like eating behaviours.

Quite simply, the food cravings you experience are unlikely the result of nutritional needs, the addictive properties of foods, or a lack of self-control. Diet mentality and the stress of dieting are the most likely causes of food cravings and addictive-like food behaviour (38,108). Research has demonstrated that dieters experience significantly more food cravings than non-dieters (109), and that cravings are often associated with boredom, stress and anxiety (110). It appears that mood and stress levels best explain cravings more than the nutritional attributes of the foods you crave (38). Until there is a greater understanding of a possible link between cravings and nutritional requirements, ditching diet mentality and managing stress is likely the best way to *relieve* your cravings.

Stress not only induces eating and influences your food choices, but food is also often used as a means of stress reduction. You may find yourself eating food for this purpose from time to time. It is completely normal, to say, reach for chocolate in times of stress or low mood. Chocolate contains polyphenols, which have been shown to reduce perceived stress and reduce the stress hormones, cortisol and adrenaline, in both highly stressed and non-stressed healthy individuals. A study even found that consumption of 40 g of dark or milk chocolate daily for two weeks was an effective way to reduce perceived stress in females (111). Whoops, I may have unintentionally enticed you to consume a slab of your favourite chocolate.

Although it's okay if you do, the reason I share this is to help you understand the role mood and stress can play in your cravings. You may choose to eat a few squares of chocolate to mitigate stress or you could explore other ways to reduce stress in your life. You could use your frequent reaching for chocolate or other food cravings as a signal that something needs to be investigated. The thing is, your food cravings are not something to fear or suppress with deprivation or food swaps, but welcomed as opportunities to explore your food preferences and eating behaviour.

If Not a Diet Overhaul, Then What?

Creating change with a perception of control or high expectations can be stressful and anxiety provoking. Although, when you release the must-achieve mentality, you can embrace change in a far gentler way: changing one habit at a time.

Changing one habit at a time may seem long-winded compared to changing your entire diet or lifestyle. However, it's the frantic rushing to create change that can sabotage your efforts and keep you trapped in the diet cycle. Even if you have serious physical ailments that you want to address, no change can guarantee your health and longevity. So, why *push through* and create change that you'll be unable to sustain? As Gretchen Rubin, author of, *The Happiness Project*, says, 'what you do every day matters more than what you do once in a while'.

By changing one habit at a time—one week or month at a time—you are less likely to feel pressured or overwhelmed. It can enable you to keep one thing in the forefront of your mind, amongst your copious responsibilities and priorities. This is important, as creating a new habit requires your full attention, just like when you first learnt to brush your teeth or to walk: you had to concentrate and be persistent in the mastery.

The same is true of any new habit you wish to establish. It requires your commitment to show up each day—to try again, and again, and again— even when you *fail*, or feel you aren't doing it right. You didn't give up on trying to brush your teeth or walk, despite the initial difficulty and failed attempts. As you learnt to walk, you repeatedly fell and got up until you mastered it. You have not failed, and you are not a failure if you forget or haven't yet mastered a new skill. Keep practising: with time it's likely to become an automatic behaviour, like brushing your teeth or walking.

Once you find yourself undertaking a new habit without much thought or resistance, you may consider embracing another habit change, if you wish. Thus, taking an approach of incremental steps to promote health and a sense of aliveness.

The habit you choose to change will depend on what you feel is your greatest priority. It needs to be a decision you make for yourself so that you are internally inspired to take action, rather than motivated by external influences. A habit change could be drinking more water, increasing the portion size of vegetables at your evening meal, mindfully eating one meal a day without distractions, or asking yourself, *do I need a second helping?* before automatically loading up your plate. Choose habits to change with the intention of experiencing a sense of aliveness and joy, rather than attempting to be a better version of yourself or to achieve a specific outcome.

If you notice resistance to a habit you'd like to form, take the time to explore whether the habit is right for you or not. Consider whether you have conflicting goals or any other reasons that are holding you back. If you feel emotional distress about a habit, debunk the thoughts that arise. Take the time to determine whether there's a deep-seated belief that's holding you back, such as, *I am not sure I am capable, I don't know if I can change,* or *I don't know whether I'm worth it.*

If a new habit you are attempting to create doesn't feel good, and that's the reason that you consistently *forget* to do it (i.e. avoid it), notice this. Simply because you've selected a habit to change doesn't mean you have to continue it no matter what. The intention is not to change your habits in the pursuit of perfection: you do not have to *push through* anything. That's because you are enough, exactly as you are in this moment: nothing needs to change unless you are inspired to do so.

Joyful Eating Principle 7.
INTUITIVELY NOURISH YOUR BODY

Let go of searching for the elusive perfect diet or attempting to achieve nutritional balance every time you eat. Relax.

Nourish your body with a variety of foods that maximise nutrition and enjoyment, and suit your lifestyle and food preferences. Find your own way to nourish your body and mind.

16

Embrace the Joy of Eating

"Joy does not come from what you do, it flows into what you do and thus into the world from deep within you."

—Eckhart Tolle

Diet culture and popular media have perpetuated a fear of the pleasure of food. The common expression, *guilty pleasure*, demonstrates how ingrained the belief that a love of food is *bad* and the culprit of weight and other health concerns. However, this cannot be further from the truth.

As I've previously explained, it's the attempting to control your eating and hunger that deteriorates your relationship with both food and your body, not the joy of eating. The belief that you're completely in control of your eating, your body and your life tends to generate tension and stress. It does more to sabotage your weight and health than enable you to *listen* to and trust your own body.

The thing is, seeking pleasure in food is innate. It is your primal drive to consume a variety of flavours and textures to ensure you are sufficiently nourished. Therefore, a desire to seek pleasure in eating is not a genetic flaw or personality fault. Your body is not a machine that you insert nutrition into, without pleasure or emotions. Scientific research would be hard pushed to sway our love affair with chocolate or the social norm of raising a glass of bubbles in celebration. Eating is meant to be a pleasurable, enjoyable and a social experience.

I find it incredibly sad when someone says that she's lost interest in food. Perhaps she does love food and yet she eats the same thing, day in day out, for fear that if she were to enjoy food, it would lead to uncontrollable weight gain.

However, devouring foods that you perceive as *naughty* or *unhealthy*, or overeating in general, are behaviours reinforced by diet culture, and are not reflective of the sensory experience of eating. The belief that you can't control yourself around certain foods is often the consequence of thoughts of what you should or should not be eating, rather than the pleasure of eating the food itself.

Taking pleasure in eating may actually minimise overeating, emotional eating and secret eating. A compelling study by a professor at Tel Aviv University in Israel, on the effect of restriction on dieters, found that when dieters were free to eat chocolate cake or another dessert every day after a balanced breakfast, they lost more weight than those on the same diet except for the morning dessert (112). It's not that chocolate cake has some magical weight loss properties, but that depriving yourself of foods you enjoy is the very thing that derails you. So, it's not your lack of willpower or self-control. Another study that examined participants' perception of chocolate cake found that associating chocolate cake with *guilt* led to a perceived reduction in control of their eating, compared to when chocolate cake was perceived as a pleasure (113).

Therefore, it is restriction and deprivation, not the pleasure of food, that may lead you to feel you cannot say 'no' to certain foods… or what you may consider to be *uncontrollable* eating behaviour. A study on food choice and the relationship to weight control concluded that "… difficulties of weight control may reflect problems with cues and motivations to eat, rather than with heightened pleasure derived from eating… individuals highly concerned with food intake and weight control may be particularly susceptible to thoughts, emotions, and situational cues that can prompt overeating and undermine their attempts to restrain eating. Repeat dieting, high day-to-day fluctuations in intakes, and attempts to enforce highly rigid control over eating all seem to be counterproductive to weight control efforts and may disrupt more appropriate food choice behaviours." (114).

If you fear enjoying food, take the time to explore your beliefs that perpetuate this fear and investigate them for truth. For example, in the past, you may have believed that:

- you don't have time to sit and enjoy food
- you have not earned the right to enjoy delicious food
- you don't deserve to enjoy food
- you can't let others see you enjoying food because of your weight
- you're too ashamed of your body or eating to enjoy food
- if you enjoy food you will gain weight, and your health will deteriorate
- it's unfair that others can enjoy food without undesirable weight repercussions

I hope you can now see that these thoughts are false. You don't control your weight. Your weight is not based on your enjoyment of food. You don't need to earn pleasure or joy—it is your human right! The labels, rules and beliefs you ascribe to food only serve to prevent you from experiencing the pleasure of eating; preventing you from moving and nourishing your body in ways that brings you deep satisfaction and joy.

Stop Depriving Yourself of Joy

Many clients I've worked with would put other people's needs before their own as a way of withholding pleasure from themselves. They believed they needed to do or be something to deserve pleasure. Yet, allowing yourself pleasure doesn't require you to be selfish or ignore other people's needs. It also doesn't imply that every single moment is about your pleasure. Rather, you cease depriving yourself of pleasure until *you've ticked all the boxes*: some arbitrary point in time when you'll have completed all your tasks, feel that you've met all your goals, or have earned pleasure.

Unfortunately, constantly prioritising other people's pleasure and happiness above your own can cause you to steal temporary moments of pleasure, with food frequently being the easiest and most accessible form of pleasure. This can lead to overeating, secret eating or emotional eating; as a result, it exacerbates a distrust of pleasure. Counterintuitively, when you allow yourself to experience pleasure without having to earn it, you are less likely to try to *steal* it in rare moments. Instead, you can enjoy each moment, or mouthful, without guilt and shame.

Resisting the pleasure of eating because you believe you need to earn it reminds me of the scene in the film, *Eat, Pray, Love,* when Elizabeth Gilbert, played by Julia Roberts, is talking with her Italian friends in a barbershop. Her friend, Luca Spaghetti, has a hilarious rant where he says, 'You feel guilty... you don't know how to enjoy yourself... you work too hard. You get burned out. Then you come home and spend the whole weekend in your pyjamas in front of the TV. But you don't know pleasure; you have to be told you've earned it.' The Italians, he goes on to say, are the masters of *il dolce far niente*, which is an Italian phrase that means 'the sweetness of doing nothing'.

You too can experience pleasure without having to change or attain anything. You can experience happiness and contentment by drawing your attention to the sensory experience of each moment and each time you eat.

You can embrace behaviour changes through an understanding of what you enjoy and how your body responds—physically, mentally and emotionally—to what you eat. Because it's not greater control over your eating that will bring you happiness and contentment, but releasing the labels, rules and beliefs that cause you to feel guilt for your eating and shame of your body.

It's entirely possible that when you embrace the pleasure of eating, you can tap into the joy of being alive. It is likely that it is this joy of aliveness that you seek through external validation and pleasure. However, joy does not originate outside of you, but from within you. You derive joy from how you interact with and how you witness the world. Joy is derived not only from the food you eat but the *way* you eat. Joy occurs when you are fully present and all your senses are alive. You can experience joy without having to change a thing, through tapping into the sensory experience of *what is*.

A client working with me told me of a day she was sitting in the lunchroom, and a colleague walked in and took a Kit-Kat chocolate bar from a donation box. Her colleague turned to her and said, 'I really shouldn't eat this'. Unlike in the past, when my client would have sympathised at being unable to *stick* to a diet, she instead replied, 'you enjoy that'. No matter what you choose to eat, enjoy it.

Joyful Eating Principle 8.
EMBRACE THE JOY OF EATING

Eat foods that you enjoy and enable you to feel
energetic and alive—physically, mentally and
emotionally—without guilt and shame.

Conclusion

When I've worked with clients through the concepts and activities presented in this book, they often say that they feel lighter—like a weight has been lifted. Although of course, no physical weight has shifted in a one-hour session, nor is that the intent, they feel the weight of their body shame and self-control releasing. And that is my intention for you in writing this book.

I sincerely hope you now feel that a weight has been lifted: that you feel a lighter, more joyful connection with food and your body. I hope that you can continue to surrender to *what is*, and fully experience each moment of your life as it unfolds.

Your relationship with food and your body will continue to evolve throughout your life. So, if you find yourself slipping back into old habits of eating mindlessly, compulsively or emotionally, rather than guilt or shame yourself, explore these behaviours with impartial curiosity. At these times you can come back to this book, or your companion Workbook or journal, to refresh your memory. You may also find it helpful to redo some of the Self-Reflection Activities. Each time you do so, you may find that you can delve deeper into the depths of your relationship with food and your body.

Furthermore, we continue to live in a world that is obsessed with appearance, weight, dieting and *healthy* eating. Therefore, the journey of tuning into your body and debunking food and diet rules does not end here. However, you now have tools to assist you in maintaining your grounding of *who you*

Conclusion

are when confronted with the diet and marketing messages that tell you that you are not good enough as you are. You *are* good enough exactly as you are—because you are.

It may be possible that the purpose of your life is not to look a specific way, or to attain arbitrary goals, but rather to witness your aliveness through experiencing each moment with your full awareness, curiosity and joy.

Acknowledgements

Writing Joyful Eating was in no way easy. It involved many years of filling notebooks with ideas, structuring those ideas, and then numerous iterations. Although at times I felt I was avoiding the hard work of writing, as I compiled the final version, it became apparent that these years enabled me to gain the clarity I now share. I am indebted to those who believed in what I had to share and encouraged me.

Immeasurable thanks to Michelle Stanton, founder of ZoneHigh and creator of 'A Day in the Zone' toolkit and workshop. Your teachings and tools altered the course of my life and inspired me to write this book.

An enormous thank you to Anna Kanowski, with whom I shared many conversations in the early conceptualisation of this book. Anna provided me with invaluable support and encouraging words.

Thank you to my husband, Rob Hutchings, who believed in me and that my message was worth sharing. After years of hearing me talk about these ideas, he too got to the point where he knew I had to write this book. He became my most prominent champion while I wrote the first complete draft. You have been incredibly accepting of my crazy ideas and ventures. You've been here beside me every step of the way, ensuring that there is joy and lightness in my every day. I love you.

I thank friends, colleagues, clients and workshop participants with whom I've discussed the concepts shared in this book. It's only through talking

Acknowledgements

with and observing others that I've been able to articulate my ideas and feel certain that what I have to share is of service.

I acknowledge Bev McBride, who introduced me to Geneen Roth's work way back when this idea was in its infancy; you are probably unaware of the catalyst you created. I deeply appreciate the feedback on the initial drafts of this book from Barry McBride and Carla Evans. Although I know you support all that I do, it was great to have your feedback. A huge thanks to Jennifer Lancaster, who edited the final version ready for publication. You ensured my work was ready to share with the world without losing my voice in the process. You have an incredible talent—thank you.

I thank my parents and uncles for providing me with an upbringing where I could be myself, never imposing rules or expectations as to the right way to be. Joy has been the only measure of success, and I thank you for instilling that in me. It's been a joy to feel my fingers move over the keyboard and see the words spill out of me, and I hope what I share brings you some joy.

Appendix 1

List of Self-Reflection Activities

Appendix 2

Principles for Joyful Eating

Appendix 3

Take Stock of Your Current Relationship with Food and Your Body

Below are statements about your health, stress, body and eating that can shed light on your relationship with food and your body. These statements are not a test, but a way to identify your priorities right now. Consider each statement and then tick the most accurate response for you currently. The response is based on how frequently the statement is true: 0 = never; 1 = occasionally; 2 = sometimes; 3 = often; 4 = always/continually.

Your health	0	1	2	3	4
I worry about my health					
I feel frustrated with my health					
I feel overwhelmed about my health issues					
Your stress	0	1	2	3	4
I think about my problems					
I experience feelings of tension and anxiety					
I feel worthless, inadequate or unimportant					

	0	1	2	3	4
I feel unhappy					
I find it hard to cope with my stress load					
I struggle to achieve work/life balance					
I rarely take time to relax and have fun					
Your weight and body	**0**	**1**	**2**	**3**	**4**
I am discontent with my current weight					
I weigh myself					
I don't purchase clothes when I don't like the size label					
My weight has fluctuated over the past 10 years					
I exercise to make up for my eating					
Your relationship with food	**0**	**1**	**2**	**3**	**4**
I am confused about how to eat healthily					
I think about food and dieting					
I have dieted					
I restrict my food intake					
I don't make time to eat or for regular meals					
I eat when I am not hungry					
I feel the need to finish everything on my plate					
I eat beyond feeling satisfied (until I'm stuffed)					
I frequently eat too much or not enough					
I eat fast					
I eat at my desk, driving, standing or in front of the TV					
I eat uncontrollably at times					
I cannot trust myself around food					
If food is delicious, I eat a second serve					
If there is a treat food in the house, I find it hard to resist					
I am tempted by foods I shouldn't eat					

Your relationship with food	0	1	2	3	4
I feel guilty after eating					
I eat when stressed					
I eat when bored					
I eat when emotional					
I am bored with my current diet					
I eat a limited range of foods					
I rarely try or experiment with new foods					

Take the time to look over your responses and observe whenever you recorded 3 and above. What do you feel is your greatest priority or concern regarding your relationship with food and your body right now? You may like to note in your Workbook or journal what issues you consider your greatest priority and any associated thoughts that arise.

On finishing this book and the Self-Reflection Activities, you may like to come back to this form and compare how things have changed. If you have the companion Workbook, you will find this form at both the beginning and end of the Workbook.

Alternatively, you could photocopy this form, so you have a copy you can complete before and after reading this book, and then compare your responses side-by-side. If you choose to photocopy this form, you could glue or staple the copies into your journal.

Bibliography

1. Keys A, Brozek J, Henschel A, Mickelsen O, Taylor HL. The Biology of Human Starvation, Vols. I-II. University of Minnesota Press, Minneapolis, MN; 1950.

2. Men Starve in Minnesota: Conscientious Objectors Volunteer for Strict Hunger Tests to Study Europe's Food Problem. Life. 1945 July 30; 19(5): p. 43-6.

3. Polivy J, Herman CP. Dieting and binging. A causal analysis. Am Psychol. 1985; 40(2): p. 193–201.

4. Prentice AM, Goldberg GR, Jebb SA, Black AE, Murgatroyd PR, Diaz EO. Physiological responses to slimming. Proc Nutr Soc. 1991; 50: p. 441–58.

5. Burke LK, Darwish T, Cavanaugh AR, Virtue S, Roth E, Morro J, et al. mTORC1 in AGRP neurons integrates exteroceptive and interoceptive food-related cues in the modulation of adaptive energy expenditure in mice. Elife. 2017; 6: p. e22848.

6. Cambridge Institute of Public Health RN. Why our brain cells may prevent us burning fat when we're dieting. 2017 May 23.

7. Hill AJ. Does dieting make you fat? Br J Nutr. 2004; 92((Suppl. 1)): p. S15-S18.

8. Pietiläinen KH, Saarni SE, Kaprio J, Rissanen A. Does dieting make you fat? A twin study. Int J Obes (Lond). 2012; 36(3): p. 456-64.

9. Goodrick GK, Poston WS, Foreyt JP. Methods for voluntary weight loss and control: update 1996. Nutrition. 1996; 12(10): p. 672-6.

10. Siahpush M, Tibbits M, Shaikh RA, Singh GK, Sikora Kessler A, Huang TT. Dieting increases the likelihood of subsequent obesity and BMI gain: results from a prospective study of an Australian national sample. Int J Behav Med. 2015; 22(5): p. 662-71.

11. Mann T, Tomiyama AJ, Westling E, Lew AM, Samuels B, Chatman J. Medicare's search for effective obesity treatments: diets are not the answer. Am Psychol. 2007; 62(3): p. 220-33.

12. Sumithran P, Prendergast LA, Delbridge E, Purcell K, Shulkes A, Kriketos A, et al. Long-term persistence of hormonal adaptations to weight loss. N Engl J Med. 2011; 365(17): p. 1597-604.

13. Rosenbaum M, Murphy EM, Heymsfield SB, Matthews DE, Leibel RL. Low dose leptin administration reverses effects of sustained weight-reduction on energy expenditure and circulating concentrations of thyroid hormones. J Clin Endocrinol Metab. 2002; 87(5): p. 2391-4.

14. MacLean PS, Higgins JA, Johnson GC, Fleming-Elder BK, Donahoo WT, Melanson EL, et al. Enhanced metabolic efficiency contributes to weight regain after weight loss in obesity-prone rats. Am J Physiol Regul Integr Comp Physiol. 2004; 287(6): p. R1306-15.

15. Dulloo AG, Jacquet J, Girardier L. Poststarvation hyperphagia and body fat overshooting in humans: a role for feedback signals from lean and fat tissues. Am J Clin Nutr. 1997; 65(3): p. 717-23.

16. Müller MJ, Bosy-Westphal A, Heymsfield SB. Is there evidence for a setpoint that regulates human body weight? F1000 Med Rep. 2010; 2: p. 59.

17. Keesey R.E. HMC. Body Weight Set-Points: Determination and Adjustment. J Nutr. 1997; 127(9): p. 1875S-1883S.

18. Leibel R.L. RM,HJ. Changes in energy expenditure resulting from altered body weight. N Engl J Med. 1995; 332: p. 621-8.

19. Redman LM, Heilbronn LK, Martin CK, de Jonge L, Williamson DA, Delany JP, et al. Metabolic and behavioural compensations in response to caloric restriction: implications for the maintenance of weight loss. PLoS One. 2009; 4(2): p. e4377.

20. Harris RB. Role of set-point theory in regulation of body weight. FASEB J. 1990; 4(15): p. 3310-8.

21. Leibel RL. Molecular physiology of weight regulation in mice and humans. Int J Obes(Lond). 2008; 32(Suppl 7): p. S98-S108.

22. Strohacker K, Carpenter KC, McFarlin BK. Consequences of Weight Cycling: An Increase in Disease Risk? Int J Exerc Sci. 2009; 2(3): p. 191–201.

23. Montani JP, Schutz Y, Dulloo AG. Dieting and weight cycling as risk factors for cardiometabolic diseases: who is really at risk? Obes Rev. 2015; 16 (Suppl 1): p. 7-18.

24. Bacon L. Health at Every Size: The Surprising Truth about Your Weight Dallas: TX BenBella Books; 2010.

25. Morris AM, Katzman DK. The impact of the media on eating disorders in children and adolescents. Paediatr Child Health. 2003; 8(5): p. 287–9.

26. Spettigue W, Henderson KA. Eating disorders and the role of the media. Can Child Adolesc Psychiatr Rev. 2004; 13(1): p. 16–19.

27. Patton GC, Selzer R, Coffey C, Carlin JB, Wolfe R. Onset of adolescent eating disorders: population based cohort study over 3 years. BMJ. 1999; 318(7186): p. 765-8.

28. O'Brien KS, Latner JD, Puhl RM, Vartanian LR, Giles C, Griva K, et al. The relationship between weight stigma and eating behavior is explained by weight bias internalization and psychological distress. Appetite. 2016; 102: p. 70-6.

29. Vartanian LR, Porter AM. Weight stigma and eating behavior: A review of the literature. Appetite. 2016; 102: p. 3-14.

30. Tomiyama AJ. Weight stigma is stressful. A review of evidence for the cyclic obesity/weight-based stigma. Appetite. 2014; 82: p. 8-15.

31. Phelan SM, Burgess DJ, Yeazel MW, Hellerstedt WL, Griffin JM, van Ryn M. Impact of weight bias and stigma on quality of care and outcomes for patients with obesity. Obes Rev. 2015; 16(4): p. 319–26.

32. Link BG, Phelan JC. Stigma and its public health implications. Lancet. 2006; 367: p. 528–29.

33. Myers A, Rosen JC. Obesity stigmatization and coping: relation to mental health symptoms, body image, and self-esteem. Int J Obes Relat Metab Disord. 1999; 23(3): p. 221–30.

34. Vartanian LR, Shaprow JG. Effects of weight stigma on exercise motivation and behavior. J Health Psychol. 2008; 13(1): p. 131–38.

35. PSC Collaborators. Body-mass index and cause-specific mortality in 900 000 adults: collaborative analyses of 57 prospective studies. Lancet. 2009; 373(9669): p. 1083–96.

36. Tomiyama AJ, Ahlstrom B, Mann T. Long-term effects of dieting: is weight loss related to health? Soc Personal Psychol Compass. 2013; 7(12): p. 861–77.

37. Tomiyama JA, Mann T, Vinas D, Hunger JM, DeJager J, Taylor SE. Low calorie dieting increases cortisol. Psychosom Med. 2010; 72(4): p. 357–64.

38. Yau YHC, Potenza MN. Stress and Eating Behaviors. Minerva Endocrinol. 2013; 38(3): p. 255–67.

39. Urbszat D, Herman CP, Polivy J. Eat, drink, and be merry, for tomorrow we diet: effects of anticipated deprivation on food intake in restrained and unrestrained eaters. J Abnorm Psychol. 2002; 111((2)): p. 396-401.

40. Berridge KC, Ho CY, Richard JM, DiFeliceantonio AG. The tempted brain eats: Pleasure and desire circuits in obesity and eating disorders. Brain Res. 2010; 1350: p. 43–64.

41. Wegner DM, Schneider DJ. "The White Bear Story". Psychological Inquiry. 2003; 14(3/4): p. 326–9.

42. World Health Organization. Basic Documents. Forty-fifth edition, Supplement ed.; 2014.

43. Bratman S. Health food junkie. Yoga J. 1997;: p. 42–50.

44. Dunn TM, Bratman S. On orthorexia nervosa: A review of the literature and proposed diagnostic criteria. Eat Behav. 2016; 21: p. 11-17.

45. Tsigos C, Kyrou I, Kassi E, Chrousos GP. Stress, Endocrine Physiology and Pathophysiology. [Updated 2016 Mar 10]. In De Groot LJ, Chrousos G, Dungan K, Feingold KR, Grossman A, Hershman JM, et al. Endotext [Internet]. South Dartmouth (MA): MDText.com, Inc.; 2000.

46. Seematter G, Binnert C, Tappy L. Stress and metabolism. Metab Syndr Relat Disord. 2005; 3(1): p. 8-13.

47. Nakamura Y, Walker BR, Ikuta T. Systematic review and meta-analysis reveals acutely elevated plasma cortisol following fasting but not less severe calorie restriction. Stress. 2016; 19(2): p. 151-7.

48. Konturek PC, Brzozowski T, Konturek SJ. Stress and the gut: pathophysiology, clinical consequences, diagnostic approach and treatment options. J Physiol Pharmacol. 2011; 62(6): p. 591-9.

49. Delvaux MM. Stress and visceral perception. Can J Gastroenterol. 1999; 13 Suppl A: p. 32A-36A.

50. Bhatia V, Tandon RK. Stress and the gastrointestinal tract. J Gastroenterol Hepatol. 2005; 20(3): p. 332-9.

51. Emond M, Ten Eycke K, Kosmerly S, Robinson AL, Stillar A, Van Blyderveen S. The effect of academic stress and attachment stress on stress-eaters and stress-undereaters. Appetite. 2016; 100: p. 210-5.

52. Gibson EL. Emotional influences on food choice: sensory, physiological and psychological pathways. Physiol Behav. 2006; 89(1): p. 53–61.

53. Wardle J, Steptoe A, Oliver G, Lipsey Z. Stress, dietary restraint and food intake. J Psychosom Res. 2000; 48(2): p. 195-202.

54. Hróbjartsson A, Gøtzsche PC. Placebo interventions for all clinical conditions. Cochrane Database Syst Rev. 2010; 1: p. 1465-858.

55. Wooley OW, Wooley SC, Dunham RB. Can calories be perceived and do they affect hunger in obese and nonobese humans? J Comp Physiol Psychol. 1972; 80(2): p. 250-8.

56. Pardi D, Buman M, Black J, Lammers GJ, Zeitzer JM. Eating decisions based on alertness levels after a single night of sleep manipulation: a randomized clinical trial. Sleep. 2017; 40(2): p. 1-8.

57. Greer SM, Goldstein AN, Walker MP. The impact of sleep deprivation on food desire in the human brain. Nat Commun. 2013; 4: p. 2259.

58. Chaput JP. Sleep patterns, diet quality and energy balance. Physiol Behav. 2014; 134: p. 86-91.

59. Strauss RS. Self-reported weight status and dieting in a cross-sectional sample of young adolescents: National Health and Nutrition Examination Survey. Arch Pediatr Adolesc Med. 1999; 153(7): p. 741-7.

60. Wansink B. Mindless Eating: why we eat more than we think: Random House USA; 2007.

61. Arch JJ, Brown KW, Goodman RJ, Della Porta MD, Kiken LG, Tillman S. Enjoying food without caloric cost: The impact of brief mindfulness on laboratory eating outcomes. Behav Res Ther. 2016; 79: p. 23-34.

62. Ahrén B, Holst JJ. The cephalic insulin response to meal ingestion in humans is dependent on both cholinergic and noncholinergic mechanisms and is important for postprandial glycemia. Diabetes. 2001; 50(5): p. 1030-8.

63. Eliasson B, Rawshani A, Axelsen M, Hammarstedt A, Smith U. Cephalic phase of insulin secretion in response to a meal is unrelated to family history of type 2 diabetes. PLoS One. 2017; 12(3): p. e0173654.

64. Lorentzen M, Madsbad S, Kehlet H, Tronier B. Effect of sham-feeding on glucose tolerance and insulin secretion. Acta Endocrinol(Copenh). 1987; 115(1): p. 84–6.

65. Maruyama K, Sato S, Ohira T, Maeda K, Noda H, Kubota Y, et al. The joint impact on being overweight of self reported behaviours of eating quickly and eating until full: cross sectional survey. BMJ. 2008; 337: p. 1091-93.

66. Otsuka R, Tamakoshi K, Yatsuya H, Wada K, Matsushita K, OuYang P, et al. Eating fast leads to insulin resistance: findings in middle-aged Japanese men and women. Prev Med. 2008; 46(2): p. 154-9.

67. Galhardo J, Hunt LP, Lightman SL, Sabin MA, Bergh C, Sodersten P, et al. Normalizing eating behavior reduces body weight and improves gastrointestinal hormonal secretion in obese adolescents. J Clin Endocrinol Metab. 2012; 97(2): p. E193–201.

68. Andrade AM, Greene GW, Melanson KJ. Eating slowly led to decreases in energy intake within meals in healthy women. J Am Diet Assoc. 2008; 108(7): p. 1186-91.

69. Angelopoulos T, Kokkinos A, Liaskos C, Tentolouris N, Alexiadou K, Miras AD, et al. The effect of slow spaced eating on hunger and satiety in overweight and obese patients with type 2 diabetes mellitus. BMJ Open Diabetes Res Care. 2014; 2(1): p. e000013.

70. Mattes RD. Physiologic responses to sensory stimulation by food: nutritional implications. J Am Diet Assoc. 1997; 97(4): p. 406-13.

71. Orrell-Valente JK, Hill LG, Brechwald WA, Dodge KA, Pettit GS, Bates JE. "Just Three More Bites": An Observational Analysis of Parents' Socialization of Children's Eating at Mealtime. Appetite. 2007; 48(1): p. 37–45.

72. Fisher JO, Birch LL. Eating in the absence of hunger and overweight in girls at 5 and 7 years. Am J Clin Nutr. 2002; 76(1): p. 226–31.

73. Moran TH, Kinzig KP. Gastrointestinal satiety signals II. Cholecystokinin. Am J Physiol Gastrointest Liver Physiol. 2004; 286(2): p. G183-8.

74. Leidy HJ, Tang M, Armstrong CL, Martin CB, Campbell WW. The effects of consuming frequent, higher protein meals on appetite and satiety during weight loss in overweight/obese men. Obesity (Silver Spring). 2011; 19(4): p. 818-24.

75. Halton TL, Hu FB. The effects of high protein diets on thermogenesis, satiety and weight loss: a critical review. J Am Coll Nutr. 2004; 23(5): p. 373–85.

76. Stull AJ, Apolzan JW, Thalacker-Mercer AE, Iglay HB, Campbell WW. Liquid and solid meal replacement products differentially affect postprandial appetite and food intake in older adults. J Am Diet Assoc. 2008; 108(7): p. 1226–30.

77. Mourao DM, Bressan J, Campbell WW, Mattes RD. Effects of food form on appetite and energy intake in lean and obese young adults. Int J Obes(Lond). 2007; 31(11): p. 1688–95.

78. Zhu Y, Hsu WH, Hollis JH. The impact of food viscosity on eating rate, subjective appetite, glycemic response and gastric emptying rate. PLoS One. 2013; 8(6): p. e67482.

79. Fuhrman J, Sarter B, Glaser D, Acocella S. Changing perceptions of hunger on a high nutrient density diet. Nutr J. 2010; 9: p. 51.

80. Galloway AT, Fiorito LM, Lee Y, Birch LL. Parental pressure, dietary patterns, and weight status in girls who are 'picky eaters'. J Am Diet Assoc. 2005.; 105(4): p. 541–48.

81. Batsell WRJ, Brown AS, Ansfield ME, Paschall GY. You will eat all of that!: A retrospective analysis of forced consumption episodes. Appetite. 2002; 38(3): p. 211–9.

82. Raghunathan R, Naylor RW, Hoyer WD. The unhealthy = tasty intuition and its effects on taste inferences, enjoyment, and choice of food products. J Mark. 2006; 70: p. 170–84.

83. Fisher JO, Birch LL. Restricting access to palatable food affects children's behavioral response, food selection and intake. Am J Clin Nutr. 1999; 69: p. 1264–72.

84. Wansink B, Chandon P. Can "low-fat" nutrition labels lead to obesity? J Mark Res. 2006; 43(4): p. 605-17.

85. Provencher V, Polivy J, Herman CP. Perceived healthiness of food. If it's healthy, you can eat more! Appetite. 2009; 52(2): p. 340-4.

86. Finkelstein SR, Fishbach A. When Healthy Food Makes You Hungry. J Consum Res. 2010; 37(3): p. 357–67.

87. Rozin P, Ashmore M, Markwith M. Lay American conceptions of nutrition: dose insensitivity, categorical thinking, contagion, and the monotonic mind. Health Psychol. 1996; 15(6): p. 438–47.

88. Bowen D, Green P, Vizenor N, Vua C, Kreuter P, Rolls B. Effects of fat content on fat hedonics: cognition or taste? Physiol Behav. 2003;(78): p. 247–53.

89. Chandon P, Wansink B. Does food marketing need to make us fat? A review and solutions. Nutr Rev. 2012; 70(10): p. 571–93.

90. Fishbach A, Dhar R. Goals as excuses or guides: the liberating effect of perceived goal progress on choice. J Consum Res. 2005; 32: p. 370–77.

91. Ramanathan S, Williams P. Immediate and delayed emotional consequences of indulgence: the moderating influence of personality type on mixed emotions. J Consum Res. 2007; 34(2): p. 212–23.

92. Chandon P, Wansink B. The biasing health halos of fast-food restaurant health claims: lower calorie estimates and higher side-dish consumption intentions. J Consum Res. 2007; 34: p. 301–14.

93. Williams P. Consumer understanding and use of health claims for foods. Nutr Rev. 2005; 63(7): p. 256-64.

94. Fernan C, Schuldt JP, Niederdeppe J. Health halo effects from oroduct titles and nutrient content claims in the context of "protein" bars. Health Commun. 2017; 33(12): p. 1-9.

95. Davis CM. Results of the self-selection of diets by young children. Can Med Assoc J. 1939; 41(3): p. 257-61.

96. Strauss S. Clara M. Davis and the wisdom of letting children choose their own diets. CMAJ. 2006; 175(10): p. 1199–201.

97. Paroche MM, Caton SJ, Vereijken CMJL, Weenen H, Houston-Price C. How infants and young children learn about food: a systematic review. Front Psychol. 2017; 8: p. 1046.

98. Veum VL, Laupsa-Borge J, Eng Ø, Rostrup E, Larsen TH, Nordrehaug JE, et al. Visceral adiposity and metabolic syndrome after very high-fat and low-fat isocaloric diets: a randomized controlled trial. Am J Clin Nutr. 2017; 105(1): p. 85-99.

99. Buchholz AC, Schoeller DA. Is a calorie a calorie? Am J Clin Nutr. 2004; 79(5): p. 899S-906S.

100. Pasquet P, Apfelbaum M. Recovery of initial body weight and composition after long-term massive overfeeding in men. Am J Clin Nutr. 1994; 60(6): p. 861-3.

101. Simon Y, Bellisle F, Monneuse MO, Samuel-Lajeunesse B, Drewnowski A. Taste responsiveness in anorexia nervosa. Br J Psychiatry. 1993; 162: p. 244–6.

102. Rothwell NJ, Stock MJ. A role for brown adipose tissue in diet-induced thermogenesis. Nature. 1979; 281: p. 31-5.

103. Joyner MA, Gearhardt AN, White MA. Food craving as a mediator between addictive-like eating and problematic eating outcomes. Eat Behav. 2015; 19: p. 98-101.

104. Pressman P, Clemens RA, Rodriguez HA. Food addiction: clinical reality or mythology. Am J Med. 2015; 128(11): p. 1165-6.

105. Sinha R, Jastreboff AM. Stress as a common risk factor for obesity and addiction. Biol Psychiatry. 2013; 73(9): p. 827-35.

106. Massey A, Hill AJ. Dieting and food craving. A descriptive, quasi-prospective study. Appetite. 2012; 58(3): p. 781-5.

107. Hill AJ, Weaver CF, Blundell JE. Food craving, dietary restraint and mood. Appetite. 1991; 17(3): p. 187-97.

108. Sunni AA, Latif R. Effects of chocolate intake on perceived stress; a controlled clinical study. Int J Health Sci (Qassim). 2014; 8(4): p. 393–401.

109. Jakubowicz D, Froy O, Wainstein J, Boaz M. Meal timing and composition influence ghrelin levels, appetite scores and weight loss maintenance in overweight and obese adults. Steroids. 2012; 77(4): p. 323-31.

110. Kuijer RG, Boyce JA. Chocolate cake. Guilt or celebration? Associations with healthy eating attitudes, perceived behavioural control, intentions and weight-loss. Appetite. 2014; 74: p. 48-54.

111. Mela DJ. Determinants of food choice: relationships with obesity and weight control. Obes Res. 2001; 9(Issue S11): p. 249S-55S.

112. Hebebrand J, Albayrak Ö, Adan R, Antel J, Dieguez C, de Jong J, et al. "Eating addiction", rather than "food addiction", better captures addictive-like eating behavior. Neurosci Biobehav Rev. 2014; 47: p. 295-306.

113. Neumark-Sztainer D, Wall M, Haines J, Story M, Eisenberg ME. Why does dieting predict weight gain in adolescents? Findings from project EAT-II: a 5-year longitudinal study. J Am Diet Assoc. 2007; 107(3): p. 448-55.

114. Ziauddeen H, Farooqi IS, Fletcher PC. Obesity and the brain: how convincing is the addiction model? Nat Rev Neurosci. 2012; 13(4): p. 279-86.

115. Zhu Y, Hsu WH, Hollis JH. The effect of food form on satiety. Int J Food Sci Nutr. 2013; 64(4): p. 385-91.

116. Ziauddeen H, Fletcher PC. Is food addiction a valid and useful concept? Obes Rev. 2013; 14(1): p. 19-28.

117. Teff KL, Levin BE, Engelman K. Oral sensory stimulation in men: effects on insulin, C-peptide, and catecholamines. Am J Physiol. 1993; 265(6 Pt 2): p. R1223–30.

118. Gearhardt AN, White MA, Potenza MN. Binge eating disorder and food addiction. Curr Drug Abuse Rev. 2011; 4(3): p. 201–7.

119. Haber GB, Heaton KW, Murphy D, Burroughs LF. Depletion and disruption of dietary fibre. Effects on satiety, plasma-glucose, and serum-insulin. Lancet. 1977; 2: p. 679–82.

120. Hong-Yan Q, Chung-Wah C, Xu-Dong T, Zhao-Xiang B. Impact of psychological stress on irritable bowel syndrome. World J Gastroenterol. 2014; 20(39): p. 14126–31.

121. Leidy HJ, Apolzan JW, Mattes RD, Campbell WW. Food form and portion size affect postprandial appetite sensations and hormonal responses in healthy, nonobese, older adults. Obesity. 2010; 18((2)): p. 293–99.

122. Mattes RD, Campbell WW. Effects of food form and timing of ingestion on appetite and energy intake in lean young adults and in young adults with obesity. J Am Diet Assoc. 2009; 109(3): p. 430–7.

123. Quick V, Nansel TR, Liu D, Lipsky LM, Due P, Lannotti RJ. Body size perception and weight control in youth: 9-year international trends from 24 countries. Int J Obes(Lond). 2014; 38(7): p. 988–94.

124. Thorens B. Neural regulation of pancreatic islet cell mass and function. Diabetes, Obes Metab. 2014; 16(Suppl 1): p. 87–95.

125. Ulrich-Lai YM, Fulton S, Wilson M, Petrovich G, Rinaman L. Stress exposure, food intake, and emotional state. Stress. 2015; 18(4): p. 381–99.

126. Wirtz PH, von Känel R, Meister RE, Arpagaus A, Treichler S, Kuebler U U, et al. Dark chocolate intake buffers stress reactivity in humans. J Am Coll Cardiol. 2014; 63(21): p. 2297-9.

127. Zhu Y, Hsu WH, Hollis JH. Increasing the number of masticatory cycles is associated with reduced appetite and altered postprandial plasma concentrations of gut hormones, insulin and glucose. Br J Nutr. 2013; 110(2): p. 384–90.

128. Blum K, Werner T, Carnes S, Carnes P, Bowirrat A, Giordano J, et al. Sex, drugs, and rock 'n' roll: hypothesizing common mesolimbic activation as a function of reward gene polymorphisms. J Psychoactive Drugs. 2012; 44(1): p. 38-55.

Further Reading

There are many books related to the topics and concepts shared in this book. Below I've listed books that were either crucial in formulating the ideas of this book, or that I'd highly recommend in progressing your journey in healing your relationship with food and your body.

Relationship with Food

Roth G. 2000. *Women, Food and God: An Unexpected Path to Almost Everything.* Scribner, New York.

Satter E. 2011. *Secrets of Feeding a Healthy Family: How to Eat, How to Raise Good Eaters, How to Cook. Kelcy Press, New York.* I'd highly recommend this book if you are interested in supporting your children, or children you work with, to form or maintain an intuitive approach to eating. You may also check out the online resources at the Ellyn Satter Institute.

Tribole E, Resch E. 2012. *Intuitive Eating: A Revolutionary Program that Works.* St. Martin's Griffin, New York.

Tribole E, Resch E. 2017. The Intuitive Eating Workbook: Ten Principles for Nourishing a Healthy Relationship with Food. New Harbinger Publications, Oakland.

Eating Disorders

Costin C, Grabb G. 2011. *8 Keys to Recovery from an Eating Disorder: Effective Strategies from Therapeutic Practice and Personal Experience.* W.W. Norton & Company, New York.

Argus W.S., Apple R.F. 2007. *Overcoming Eating Disorders: A Cognitive-Behavioral Therapy Approach for Bulimia Nervosa and Binge-Eating Disorder (Treatments That Work).* Oxford University Press, Oxford.

Embracing the Now and Releasing Sabotaging Thoughts

Brown B. 2014. *I thought it was just me (but it isn't): telling the truth about perfectionism, inadequacy, and power.* Gotham Books, New York.

Katie B. 2003. *Loving What Is: Four Questions That Can Change Your Life.* Three Rivers Press, New York.

Tolle E. 2004. *The Power of Now: A Guide to Spiritual Enlightenment.* Namaste Publishing, Vancouver.

Tolle E. 2008. *A New Earth: Awakening to Your Life's Purpose.* Penguin, London.

Hawkins D.R. 2015. *Healing and Recovery.* Hay House, California.

Stanton M. 2006. *The Timeless World: Debunk your fears and Discover Heaven on Earth.* Starburst Publishing, Adelaide.

Stanton M. 2009. *Selling in the Zone: Stress Free Success in Sales.* Tish'n Enigma Books, South Australia.

Novels

Perhaps you don't feel you require any more theory or practise than you've received in this book. Instead, you may like to read a relaxing and entertaining novel that also enables you to reflect on the principles presented in this book. If so, you may enjoy reading:

Van Praag M. 2013. *Men, Money and Chocolate: What more could there be to life?* Hay House, London.

Ahern C. 2014. *The Time of My Life.* Harper Collins, Sydney.

Plus, I have a novel coming out in 2022, *The Weight of a Woman*, a fictional story of a woman going through a journey of self-acceptance as in this book. Find out more at: www.joyfuleatingnutrition.com/novels

Resources

Companion Workbook

A Companion Workbook is available in PDF format, which you can download and print, enabling you to easily fill in the Self-Reflection Activities presented in this book. Download your free copy at www.joyfuleatingnutrition.com/book.

Body Scan Meditation

You can download an audio *body scan* meditation to relax your body and quieten your mind at www.joyfuleatingnutrition.com/book. This is designed to initiate the relaxation response and draw your awareness to *what is,* as experienced through your five senses of sight, sound, smell, taste and touch.

Index

Made in United States
Orlando, FL
29 January 2023

29196229R00164